Queer and Trans Voices:

*Achieving Liberation Through*

*Consistent Anti-Oppression*

J. FELIZ BRUECK & Z. McNEILL

An LGBTQIA+ Vegan Community Project

## Sanctuary Publishers

Sanctuary Publishers, www.SanctuaryPublishers.com

-A Book Publisher That Gives Back-

Every book sold supports marginalized communities.

Cover Design by Danae Silva Montiel
Cover Image by RawPixel.com/Freepik

\*\*\*

This book is intended as general information only. Although every effort has been taken to ensure that the information is accurate, each person's health and dietary needs are unique. Therefore, a qualified health care provider should always be consulted. This book is sold with the understanding that the authors, editors, and publisher shall have neither liability nor responsibility for any injury caused or alleged to be caused directly or indirectly by the information contained in this book.

# DEDICATION

To all the lives lost, human and nonhuman, and all those we will lose before humans finally recognize that liberation for *some* excludes others.

To Black, Brown, and Indigenous Trans Womxn – thank you for allowing us to live closer to our authentic-selves decades after fighting to be able to live yours.

To everyone that has taken a chance on Sanctuary Publishers, we're not done just yet!

# CONTENTS

**Acknowledgments**                                    i

**Preface**                                            1

1   **Introduction**                                   11

2   **Reflections from the LGBTQIA+ Vegan Community:**   33
    **Interconnections**

*Climate Catastrophe, Animal Agriculture, and the
World's Marginalized Communities*
By Chris H.

*Oppressive Dichotomies:
Fighting for Animals with Queer Liberation*
By Moe Constantine

*It's Not Because I'm Vegan*
By Brooke Shephard

*A Hierarchy That Should Not Exist*
By R.S.

*Love Isn't Scarce*
By Jocelyn Ramírez

*The American Pipe Dream*
By Grayson Black

*Trans-cending the 'Man' and the Meat-Eater*
By Doel Rakshit

*Dual Identities: Feminist, Vegan, and LGBTQIA+*
By Kanika Sud

*On Being (Un)Natural:*
*Queer Veganism and the Appeal to Nature*
By S. Marek Muller

*Let's Go Outside:*
*Thoughts on Queer Veganism*
By Margaret Robinson

*Suffering from Oppression, We Oppress*
By Janine Fuentes

*First Vegan, Then Homo?*
By Agnieszka Rahela Olszak

*Breaking Through*
By Karla Galvez

*One White Queer's Thoughts:*
*The Animal Welfare Movement*
By Anonymous

*Toward an Anti-Carceral Queer Veganism*
By Leah Kirts

*Beyond Binaries:*
*An Interspecies Case for They/Them Pronouns*
By Patti Nyman

*Queer Vegan Politics and Consistent Anti-Oppression*
By Shiri Eisner

*Is Your Memory Long Enough for the Road Ahead?*
*The Problem with Inclusion*
By LoriKim Alexander

3    **Conversations with Activists**                    275

Jasmin Singer

Z. Griffler

Michelle Carrera

Suzy González

Margaret Robinson

Lilia Trenkova

Ikora Rey

4    **A Final Note**                                    323

5    **About the Contributors**                          327

6    **About Sanctuary Publishers**                      337

# ACKNOWLEDGMENTS

In April of 2019, I contacted Sanctuary Publishers concerning a community project I had been meditating on for a while. I had read *Veganism of Color* and *Veganism in an Oppressive World* and was more impacted by those collections than any other vegan/animal rights book that I had ever read. Reading the words "white veganism is white supremacy" also led me to face my whiteness, internalized racism, and relationship to white supremacy not only in the vegan movement but in every space I occupied. Doing the work of actually being an accomplice instead of just performing superficial allyship as a white queer vegan was the first step for me to really *do* veganism.

The more I learned about Julia and their work—a myriad of social justice and community building projects centering queer and trans Black, Brown, Indigenous People of Color, dismantling neuroableism, and giving space to Vegans of Color—the more I recognized the importance of being consistently against all forms of oppression. It is continual labor with no "congratulations" at the end, but it is the only way to create true continuous change. I would like to challenge other white vegans to do the work (Layla F. Saad's *Me and White Supremacy Workbook* is a great place to start) and for non-vegan queer folks to include nonhuman animals in their repertoire of activisms.

I, along with Julia, would like to thank the contributors in this collection for doing the labor of exploring the interconnections between their queer identity and their vegan activism. I hope that you, the reader, will leave with the understanding that oppressions are interconnected and thus, to fight for queer liberation, you must also fight for nonhuman animal liberation, vice versa, and beyond.

By purchasing this collection, you are making a political impact. All sales of this book will go back into the community and directly support queer and trans BBIPoC. We're grateful for your support but hope that you will use this collection as a starting point for your toolkit towards collective liberation. I hope that you feel empowered to be the change and ripple-effect out into the world.

In Solidarity,

Z. Zane McNeill

# PREFACE

## *Zane*

When I was 15, I took my crush into the woods near my house and asked them if they would like to date me. It was uncomfortably humid, and I remember being so nervous and sweaty. She, like many of my friends in the Bible Belt of West Virginia, was raised by very religious grandparents who were trying to compensate for the abandonment of their grandchildren by their children. Their children were victims of the opioid epidemic, and these grandparents thought the only way to prevent a reoccurrence of that was strictness. She was told every day that being gay was a sin. Her grandparents would view her being gay as another one of their failures—first, their children falling to addiction and, now, their grandchild falling to a different sin through their queerness.

My crush was also vegan and chronically ill. Her grandparents believed that her being vegan was causing her illness and would tell her every day that if she ate meat, eggs, and dairy, she would be healthy again. They tolerated her diet but didn't try to understand the reasons why she *chose* at 11 to be vegan – strong ethics against violence towards animals. Her family saw veganism as a phase that she would grow out of.

Her vegan-ness and queerness isolated her from her family. She was relegated to her room when they cooked food for dinner that she couldn't eat because they refused to make her vegan options. While she nervously accepted to date me, she was adamant that no one find out. So I would come over after school when her family wasn't there, holding her hand in the basement where no one could see.

I'm not sure where she is now, almost ten years later. I'm not sure if she accepted her queerness and became a queer liberation activist or continued with her veganism and continued to fight for animal and human rights. But I know where I stand a decade later and why.

My story mirrors hers. I went vegetarian when I was 11 and vegan when I was 14. I was drawn to animal rights activism because it exists at the intersections of injustices that I oppose – those of global climate change, environmental racism, farm worker struggles, and non-human animal abuse. As a white, often cis-read, person with academic privilege, I am in a place where I am able to fight for a future that prioritizes the liberation of the most marginalized in our communities. Adding to my story, I came out as bi at 15 to my friends and four years later, for the second time, to my family. I then came out as nonbinary at 21 and am currently moving towards socially and medically transitioning.

I was raised by an ecofeminist who read the likes of Greta Gaard, Carol Adams, and Alice Walker. Thus, the basis of my understanding of the interconnections between environmental justice, veganism, and queer theory were gifted to me through my mother's personality and identity as it flowed into me. In college, I explored these theorists myself and extended my interest from veganism to food sovereignty and food justice. During my mistaken period studying for a Master of Arts degree in political science, I fell into gender studies and fell in love with queer theory, queer ecologies, and justice movements that prioritized consistent anti-oppression, the act of working against *all* oppression and exploitation.

I felt like I had finally been given the tools to create a better future that centered the most oppressed, particularly across justice movements that had historically centered the most privileged across their platforms. I recognized that although most theoretical works have been written by white people, the most transformative *real work* has been and is being done by Black people, especially Black Queer People of Marginalized Genders (MaGe). This gap in theory isn't because MaGe aren't writing ecofeminist work but because their voices are marginalized in academia just as in larger society. This trend mirrors the disparity in the vegan and animal rights movement in general. White cis men and women are given platforms that eclipse MaGe who are creating the most revolutionary change.

### *Julia*

I remember the first time I heard the word *lesbian*; I was sitting in the back seat of my grandma's car as a child. I can't remember why, but this was the moment my grandmother warned me of them: "stay away from *lesbians*; they are possessive, jealous, and they will murder you if you don't reciprocate their romantic interest." I didn't know what a lesbian actually was, but they sounded scary and not anyone I ever wanted to run into for my safety.

I was born and raised on the island of Puerto Rico to an Afro-Dominican father and a light-skinned Puerto Rican mother in the '80s. My experiences with what defined queerness came from a culture not at all ready to even speak of such things unless to discourage them, deny them, or instill fear in them. I can't remember the exact moment I became conscious of what gay or lesbian meant (at the time, this was the only language available to define queerness), but I remember, in middle school, praying that I was not gay every time that I would ask myself if I could possibly have feelings for a girl. I became numb by suppressing any thought deeply into an internal abyss that would take decades to resurface.

Eventually, Ricky Martin, a famous and beloved Puerto Rican singer known across the world, would come out as a gay man, and this would help culminate acceptance within my culture on the tiny island where I was born; however, this acceptance seemed to only extend to famous gay men, and thus, it was not enough to change perceptions of queerness as a whole and for me to truly embrace what I suppressed deep down inside of me. I'd go through my teen and college years regretfully and blushingly turning down any invitations outside of the designated path and the life I was meant to live as a "good," well-behaved, conservative Latin girl that did everything by the book, as expected.

Moving as a pre-teen to the mainland U.S. didn't make things any easier. "They are just confused and lost" was a sentiment I heard often about my openly queer peers. I also remember a friend suddenly disappearing never to be seen again after coming out when we were 15; this was Florida in the late '90s. I still think of her often; I tend to catch myself wondering what the consequences may have been for her daring to live as her authentic self at such a young age. In essence, up to that point in my life, I had experienced the reality for people like myself within two countries and a mix of cultures whose influences molded me. All messages confirmed, in agreement, that queerness, in any form, for non-cis men, was not acceptable.

Memories of fleeting instances are the only things that I have now as I head into another decade of life to work through the unspoken rules of assimilation. I can account for experiences, conversations, and instances growing up, which enforced white, cis, straight, and neurotypical as the way to be. I remember a story told to me about my Dominican father in which he had a patient refuse to be treated by him upon seeing my father. I remember not understanding the person's behavior or the implication of the story. It's only recently, as an adult actively seeking decolonization and after experiencing continuous overtly and covertly forms of racism in the U.S. and Europe, that I realized what that actually meant. Just like I had been indirectly taught to hide my queerness, "blanquiamento" (racial whitening) on the island meant that I had been unconsciously taught to hide my Blackness despite the melanin in my skin, through a rhetoric that romanticized African cultures as part of our very distant history and influences while teaching me to hide that I am part of the African diaspora through the elevation of our European colonialist history (Rivera-Rideau 2015). See, my father was a Black Dominican man on an island that has been taught, through racial castes implemented through Spanish rule and U.S. imposed (yet made to believe doesn't exist by the most privileged), racial hierarchies that whiteness is the goal through mixing, reframing our identity, and assimilation. This, while claiming racial democracy and experiencing violence from the mainland U.S. for not being white. It's not that I, or we, do not know we are African; it's that "the Spanish contributed to the production of racial hierarchies that valorized whiteness and demonized blackness...the silencing of blackness and of racism continued after 1898...," the year Puerto Rico became a U.S. colony. In essence, the culture had learned to assimilate to the expected colonial whitening by acknowledging its African and Indigenous ancestry yet prioritizing its ties to our European past and newly acquired Americanization (Rivera-Rideau 2015).

Going further through my identities, I can remember the moment in which I felt shame for the first time for my neurodivergence; this experience unconsciously resulted in my choosing to remain silent about my thoughts and needs for well into my third decade of life. When Kimberlé Crenshaw spoke of intersecting oppressions that add up to an individual based on their interconnected identities, I was able to find a tool that allowed me to trace my identities and how they have interacted with one another as well as the choices I have made or have been made for me to keep me safe in an intolerant, supremacist society. However, Crenshaw's theory also allowed me to understand where I hold privileges. Acknowledging my privileges over others allowed me to know when and how to take action to raise the voices of others and to carve out space for them when my privileges would protect me in doing so.

It took a special, young person in my life, part of my family, to come out to me to make me realize that, just maybe, my time had come – maybe it was finally safe - even with the very real possibility that my mother, raised by the same woman that cultivated fear of myself as a child, would disown me. I had privilege in this situation, and I wanted to make sure the next generation of my family would never feel the need to hide their authentic self out of fear just to feel loved and accepted. I had already started the process of self-acceptance and decolonization, and I decided to take this last leap for myself and them. I believe that waiting actually saved and empowered me. As someone born in the '80s, times have markedly moved on, and as soon as I came out to the world, I was able to piece together *all* of my identity – unapologetically and loudly using their privileges to create change in a world committed to assimilation.

I'm a neurodivergent, gendervague (nonbinary), pansexual, queer Afro-Indigenous Boricua (Puerto Rican) whose path had crossed with veganism at the intersection of their queerness, neurodivergence, and race. It all seemed to happen at once. I rejected social norms that dictated parts of me, including my ethics, as "wrong," refused to walk on the designated path that had silenced my whole life, started to decolonize myself, and challenged myself to acknowledged that privilege is a powerful tool we all have to dismantle hierarchies and oppressions.

Over a decade after embracing veganism and non-human animal rights, I affirm that the concept of intersectionality helped me make sense of my experiences and identities. As a Brown Person of Marginalized Gender (MaGe; coined by Crystal Michelle), I realized that I needed to work on taking down my role in the oppressions of others as a whole. Centering Black people of marginalized genders, especially Black Trans People of MaGe, and addressing my internalized anti-blackness became givens. Having privilege in not being read as a fully Black or fully Indigenous person through my lighter Brown skin means I do not experience the full extent of hardships that fully Black or Indigenous communities experience on the mainland U.S. and Europe, for example. Recognizing this does not take away from my own struggles and oppressions. It simply means that when I can, I do what I can to use that to make things better for my communities and shake systems of oppression to work towards dismantling them. This is the same for my neurodivergence, in which my inattentiveness helps mask it in many situations, as well as in my non-binary identity in which I am read as femme despite not identifying as a woman. These things are forms of privilege that have helped keep me safer in certain situations that others are not.

A lesser spoken form of privilege, I have human animal privilege over a system that automatically deems nonhuman animals as "less than." About a decade ago, at 25, I went vegan after realizing what this system entailed and what it meant. At this same time, I fell hard for a girl for the first time in my life; she also happened to be the first vegan I had ever met, and, oh, how times have changed...

*** 

In the radical fashion of *Sanctuary Publishers*, whose published work continues to focus on the importance of dismantling *all* systems of oppression and uplifting the most marginalized in our communities, the chapters within the subsequent pages continue this tradition by giving space to LGBTQIA+ vegans, especially Trans and Queer Black, Brown, and Indigenous People of Color, who face compounded marginalization for being queer.

Similar to the stories of our own queer journeys, which were interlaced with the uncovering of our intersecting identities, struggles, realizations, and

9

eventually, a firm commitment to consistent anti-oppression beyond a species binary, this anthology features the narratives of trans and queer vegans around the world. Some of the essays explore the relationship of LGBTQIA+ persons within cis-heterosexual society as an LGBTQIA+ person, while others feature narratives exploring how LGBTQIA+ folk exist in vegan spaces, how being vegan influences their queer politics and vice versa, and how being vegan affects their relationship with non-vegan LGBTQIA+ people.

Importantly, this community-led project, which includes the words of activists, scholars, artists, students, and many others simply living their authentic selves, attempts to build bridges between the LGBTQIA+ movement and nonhuman animal rights movement through the exploration of how liberation is one that must include all – not just some.

Julia Feliz Brueck
Z. Zane McNeill

# 1 INTRODUCTION

## Veganism Through a Queer Lens

The Vegan Society, founded by the person that coined the term "vegan" in 1944, proclaims that it "may have been established 75 years ago but veganism has been around much longer. Evidence of people choosing to avoid animal products can be traced back over 2,000 years... (The Vegan Society 2019)." Veganism is usually defined as an individual abstaining from animal products because of ethical concerns and may include environmental and health-related reasons, as well. This is the shallow veganism that most people have heard of and one practiced by the mainstream majority. Although seldomly given a platform, vegans from marginalized communities, specifically Black and Indigenous vegans, affirm that veganism is one key aspect of social justice needed to destabilize the same oppressive systems that keep us bound to it as marginalized people through the use of the otherization of nonhuman animal exploitation (Feliz Brueck 2019).

If we trace the term through the last few decades, we find that veganism seems to have gained popularity in the '60s and '70s with the rise of alternative food systems like organic gardening while in the '80s, it became associated with straight-edge punk and anarchist subcultures. In the past decade, veganism has been seen as the "cool new fad," losing its political past in its assimilation to mainstream, capitalist society. The current message of the movement uncovers its ties to capitalism through commonly heard sentiments focused on "voting with our dollars" to make the world a better place. Unfortunately, this neoliberal claim merely assimilates the movement further into an established system of oppression that marginalizes low-income folks, Black Brown Indigenous People of Color (BBIPOC), and queer folks.

We would be remiss to ignore the very fact that while veganism is not a new concept, it is one that was named under the premise of ethics by white, cis men in the U.K. during a time when the second World War raged on, Jim Crow laws and segregation was in full force within the U.S., and homosexuality was illegal in the U.S. and U.K. The Vegan Society explains, "Fast forward to 1806 CE and the earliest concepts of veganism are just starting to take shape, with Dr William Lambe and Percy Bysshe Shelley amongst the first Europeans to publicly object to eggs and dairy on ethical grounds." It would be many decades later until slavery in the U.S. and U.K. would become abolished, 1865 and 1833, to be exact. As for homophobia, at the time of this writing, the U.S. has no federal law outlawing discrimination against LGBTQIA+ people while in the U.K., discrimination against lesbians and gay men was made illegal only in 2007. At this current time in history, many marginalized groups are still fighting for rights they have never had or were just barely given, and still The Vegan Society and reports of its history do not mention interconnected oppressions tied to nonhuman animal exploitation nor co-occurring systems of oppression interlaced within its history.

When we look at the history of the movement, we see that veganism was a concept that, despite already existing in other cultures and countries (Timmins 2017), became coined by a privileged community based in one of the most violent world colonizers. This cemented its path towards becoming the single-issue movement it has become at this point in time – one that remains centered on the most privileged and continues to lag in its end goal because of it. The Vegan Society (2019) notes that the term "vegan" was defined as "the principle of the emancipation of animals from exploitation by *man*," which was then amended to a definition that was defined as "to seek an end to the use of animals by *man*, food, commodities, work, hunting, vivisection, and by all other uses involving exploitation of animal life by *man* (The Vegan Society 2019)." The definition fails to mention that *man* – white, cis, colonizers – was and is still meant to encompass the very same people that introduced animal agriculture and exploitation through colonialism and then used these same species (nonhumans) to uphold societies centered on white supremacy and all other "-isms" including homo-phobia and transphobia.

## Animal Agriculture: Colonialism and the Extension of Oppression

In her paper examining the role of milk and animal colonialism, law professor Matilde Cohen (2017) explained that,

> *Across time and space, colonists used animals to conquer ecosystems and their inhabitants, from Christopher Columbus who transported horses, cattle, swine, sheep, and*

*goats to Caribbean islands to French settlers who brought cattle to New France starting in 1617, to Dutch settlers who exported their first cows to New York in 1629, to the British who landed with their sheep and bovines on the shores of Australia and New Zealand in the Eighteenth and Nineteenth Centuries. Similar in these disparate endeavors was the idea that the importation of European animals and the destruction of local fauna, flora, and local foodways were justified by the goal of "improving" agriculture and population health. Animals and their "products"—in particular milk, leather, fur, bone, wool, and silk—were and remain constitutive of national identity and imperial power. They operate as tools of domination to control territories, humans, animals, and ecosystems. Animal colonialism also served as a pretext for conquest itself: as the imported cattle multiplied, more grazing land was needed, justifying further expansions.*

The expansion continued, and specifically within the past fifty years, nonhuman animal production has become increasingly industrialized within the United States (Holt 2008). The majority of people do not recognize the ties of colonialism with animal agriculture, and, instead, many imagine the industry as green fields and red barns filled with small numbers of nonhumans lovingly cared for by farmers. This image is but an illusion that helps society ignore the violence and history of the industry as well as the way modern agriculture has become dominated by monocultures, particularly corn and soybean production used primarily as feed for livestock consumption (Kolbe 2007).

In addition, the reality of modern nonhuman farming means row after row of large warehouses filled with thousands upon thousands of confined animals known as intensive farming operations or concentrated feeding operations (CAFOs) (Kolb 2013). These industrialized factory farms were the answer to the early 20th century need for "abundant and cheap food" for the increasing Western population (Vock and Buller 2013). This was an "answer" to a solution brought upon by colonialism, which had destroyed Indigenous society and the native environment on which they depended on.

Neoliberalism, a system that turns every person into a commodity to support free-market capitalism, severely altered all components of human life—from eroding the notion of democracy, to influencing something as personal as the food we eat and from where it comes. The industrialization of animal agriculture, in particular, has led to global inequalities and mass environmental degradation.

U.S. animal welfare movements have attempted to curb the factory farming industry's mostly unregulated power, but their consumer-oriented solution to global climate change and inequality poses problems. Subsequent industrialization, then, provided a "low cost source of meat, milk, and eggs, due to [the] efficient feeding and housing of animals" (Kolb 2013) to *man* – the very same racial majority that The Vegan Society claimed and still claims seeks an end to the use of animals in a system that forced our dependency on their exploitation. This liberalization of trade has subsequently altered the global agricultural system and, as Alkon and Mares (2012) contend, a "corporate food regime." In essence, nonhuman agriculture coupled with capitalism are mere forced extensions of colonization in the same way that gender binarism, homophobia, and transphobia are also extensions of this same oppressive system forced on "new lands" hundreds of years ago. Oppressive supremacist attitudes and ideologies brought from Europe ignored the relationships that Indigenous people had with their natural environment. One cannot acknowledge their impacts as settlers, descendants of white immigrants, in modern times without acknowledging how supporting animal agriculture is merely an extension of this very system. At the same time, People of Color cannot truly decolonize without acknowledging and rejecting the very system that utilized other animals and their forced agriculture as a tool of violent colonization and expansion.

## Otherization and Its Cognitive
## Socialized Justification

Before colonialism by Europeans, Indigenous communities recognized five genders: female, male, two-spirit female, two-spirit male, and trans-gendered, which they named in their own languages (Williams 2016). The Indian Health Service (2019) defines two-spirit as:

> *Traditionally, Native American two spirit people were male, female, and sometimes intersexed individuals who combined acti-vities of both men and women with traits unique to their status as two spirit people. In most tribes, they were considered neither men nor women; they occupied a distinct, alternative gender status. In tribes where two spirit males and females were referred to with the same term, this status amounted to a third gender.*

While the term is reserved for Indigenous communities, it can be said that it is comparable to the term "nonbinary" currently used in the mainstream LGBTQIA+ community (Deerinwater 2018).

Tasha Williams (2019) noted that Indigenous members were valued for their contribution to society rather than their gendered identity or whom they loved. This all changed through Christian enforced gender roles defined solely by "male" or "female." Therefore, through time, colonization actively ensured the erasure of two-spirit people and any other gender outside the modernly held binary through forced assimilation by white Europeans. The Indian Health Service (2019) further explains, "The disruptions caused by conquest and disease, together with the efforts of missionaries, government agents, boarding schools, and white settlers resulted in the loss of many traditions in Native communities. Two spirit roles, in particular, were singled out for condemnation, interference, and many times violence. As a result, two spirit traditions and practices went underground or disappeared in many tribes."

Along the same vein, Bernardine Evaristo (2014) explains that, "...like everywhere else, African people have expressed a wide range of sexualities. Far from bringing homosexuality with them, Christian and Islamic forces fought to eradicate it. By challenging the continent's indigenous social and religious systems, they helped demonize and persecute homosexuality in Africa, paving the way for the taboos that prevail today." In essence, before Western colonialism, traditional African cultures around the continent were tolerant of diverse sexual relationships and gender roles beyond a male-female binary and "straight-only" relations (Kalende 2014). Particularly, British colonial rule imposed severe laws that criminalized these normalized traditions during pre-colonial times driven by "New ruling-class ideas in Europe about the existence of a distinct group of diseased "homosexuals" mixed with racist conceptions of Africans. Since colonial writers perceived Africans as *"uncivilized and close to nature,"* they also saw them as incapable of exerting control over their *natural "heterosexual instincts."* Consequently, according to Han and O'Mahoney (2018), "The British Empire drafted these penal codes with a moral, religious mission in mind. The intention was to protect local Christians from 'corruption' and correct and Christianize 'native' custom." Disturbingly, the same authors published research that "provides systematic evidence" that anti-gay laws that persist to this day around the world were directly inherited from colonial criminalization (Han and O'Mahoney 2014).

As discussed in the anthology *Veganism of Color* (Feliz Brueck 2019), "White supremacy, through colonialism, successfully implemented hierarchies not just between the "races" they classified us into (some which it forcibly created) but between humans and non-human animal species as well. This specific hierarchy between species made it possible to create a divide between our own communities and the natural world." Race, however, wasn't the only hierarchy used to further fragment colonized communities. As has been established, gender and sexuality were also targeted under colonial destruction. White, cis European settlers enforced their white (pseudo) supremacist status over Indigenous and African communities through their otherization and implied proximity through *animalization* to the natural world. Therefore, an extension of colonialism, society has taught us to internalize the notion that exploiting nonhuman animals, beings even lower on the (pseudo) supremacist hierarchy, beyond necessity is just, normal, and required in a world were nonhumans were used to justify the colonization of European-designated racialized groups and subsequently, minority groups within these communities. As a result, homophobia, transphobia, queerphobia, and nonbinaryphobia took root in communities where they did not exist, and they still persist along with other forms of discrimination against all other communities (disabled, neurodivergent, etc...) deemed uncivilized and/or "below" within violently enforced white and cis standards.

Cognitive dissonance, as explained by Dr. Muller (2019), "...refers to an individual's response to contradictory thoughts/values. The oppositional thoughts/values are then responded to by either (1) justifying one's own actions so the contradiction is lessened (i.e. the problem isn't really a problem) or (2) making some kind of behavioral change to alleviate the problem." Morally contradictory phenomena like viewing something as acceptable, such as loving animals, while another related action can be seen as deviant, such as not eating animals, can result in cognitive dissonance (Muller 2019). Along with neoliberalism, morally contradictory phenomena can work jointly to block the human feeling of being connected to, and a part of, the natural world. Thereby, both result in the creation of a human-centric hierarchy that gives humans justification to domination and degrade the natural world.

How did society get here? How does society continue to justify nonhuman exploitation when it's been established that the animal agricultural industry, including factory farms, are a human health hazard, breed diseases, contaminate water, damage ecosystems, and more? Factory farms and slaughterhouse operations are a high-risk environment for workers, present ethical issues surrounding the intensive housing systems of farmed animals, and globally have led to higher social and cultural inequalities. To increase efficiency and profit, thousands of animals are kept in horrendous conditions. Cudworth notes, "In industrialized modes of slaughter, technologies have maximized the speed and ease of killing" (2015). In slaughterhouses, cruelty against animals is "systematic and normative." Yet the systems involved in factory farming are "regularized" and seen as "legitimate" (Cudworth 2015) even when the industry itself is one of the biggest exploiters of marginalized and vulnerable communities, primarily Black and Indigenous people, including undocumented migrants.

Cognitive dissonance further coupled with social constructionism, an idea that has been created and accepted as truth in society may be explanations to how oppressive systems interlocked with one another persist and are supported by the very groups most oppressed by them. Following colonization, gender and sexual diversity became unacceptable within societies that previously understood them as part of their communities. In the same way, animalization became normalized and accepted as a way for these same communities to oppress their own. Lastly, nonhuman animal exploittation, was embraced and upheld as a societal norm. Thus, the supremacist hierarchy with white and cis as the model way to be prevailed followed by other racial groups, marginalized groups within these, and then nonhuman animals, respectfully. Oppression and choosing to actively partake in the oppression of others became an accepted truth that persists to this day.

## Consistent Anti-Oppression and Veganism as Queer Politics

While justifiably invested in breaking down a specific form of supremacy on the behalf of nonhuman victims (speciesism), mainstream veganism is primarily driven by a single lens viewed by the most privileged in a hierarchical society. Mainstream (white, cis,...) veganism has managed to flip the script within a speciesist supremacist hierarchy. However, it has done so while ensuring the most privileged remain at the top – white, cis, male, able-bodied, straight, and human – while moving nonhumans up the supremacist ladder above marginalized groups. In essence, mainstream veganism prioritizes the violence perpetrated against nonhuman animals above all other marginalized peoples without recognizing how our speciesist society also harms the environment, slaughterhouse workers (many of whom are Black, Brown, Indigenous People of Color and/or immigrants in the U.S.), low-income communities who live near factory farms and suffer from health issues connected to them, etc., and how the most privileged have historically harmed now vulnerable communities, including LGBTQIA+ people, while proclaiming these same groups are now responsible ethically to undo the harm against this *one* chosen group.

Truthfully, most movements miss the opportunity to address systems of oppression by failing to embrace *consistent anti-oppression* (Feliz Brueck 2017) across all movements since all systems of oppression are inherently connected to each other. The same is true within the vegan/nonhuman animal rights movement: to fight against speciesism, the idea that humans are superior to nonhuman animals and can use them at will, we must also fight against white supremacy, environmental climate change, capitalism, and so forth. In their essay examining capitalism, colonialism, and nonhuman animal exploitation, author Shahada Chowdhury (2019) explains, "The economic and political complexities surrounding our everyday lives are easy to dismiss if one benefits from such injustices and oppression. The reality is that there is no ethical consumption under capitalism because all labor is exploited by the ruling class who profit from it. However, this does not give one free reign over perpetuating or upholding the capitalist system and, therefore, siding with oppressive forces."

It's been argued that veganism must fight against all systems of oppression—including white supremacy and cis-heteropatriarchy (Feliz Brueck 2019 ). Importantly, we must recognize the inter-section between speciesism and homophobia and transphobia through the centering of Black, Brown, and Indigenous queer liberation (New Pride Flag 2019) next to gay and trans liberation since these groups, through compounded oppressions, are even more vulnerable as they are murdered at higher rates and have less access to resources than white members of the same communities. Through the recognition of *cisheteropatriarchal speciesism*, which explores how transphobia and homophobia "animalizes" LGBTQIA+ people by excluding LGBT people as the "other" in addition to normalizing violence against other animals, the LGBTQIA+ movement can begin to work consistently against a common system rooted in our own marginalization.

In her chapter "Re/Considering Animals: A Black Woman's Journey," in *Veganism of Color* (Feliz Brueck 2019), Nekeisha Alexis writes that speciesism is part of "mutually constituting and reinforcing" systems of oppression that creates a binary between the 'normal' (white, male, human, straight, cisgender) and the 'abnormal' (Black, woman/female, non-human, queer, and trans)." Additionally, then, it can be argued that the imposed binary "create[s] lethal consequences for all of us, across species" and additionally targets deviant genders and sexualities that are seen as non-normative and in need of being controlled. In essence, Alexis builds on Greta Gaard's trans-formative essay, "Toward a Queer Ecofeminism" which argued that Western society is built on a hierarchy of dualisms that devalue the "feminized" as deviant and lesser-than (Plumwood 1991). If queer is seen as "against nature" and veganism is seen as unnatural as well, both deviant sexualities and diets are viewed as *queer* (Gaard 1997). In choosing to be vegan and embracing the politics associated with veganism, an individual is not only destabilizing the violent food system but also the other normative power structures that it symbolizes.

If, as Carol Adams (1990) has argued in her book *The Politics of Meat*, meat consumption is inherently connected to toxic masculinity, then being vegan is also "taking a stance against patriarchal culture" (Simonsen 2012). Therefore, to be vegan is also a way in which to resist heteronormativity (Simmonsen 2012) and thus *cisheteropatriarchal speciesism*. Because of this, it can be further stated that veganism not only destabilizes gendered politics but also oppressions such as racism and capitalism. Adriana Rodriguez, author of "'Strange Coupling': Vegan Ecofeminism and Queer Ecologies in Theory and in Practice," states that "...food practices regarding nonhuman animals should not reproduce other social/cultural/economic/ideological structures of oppression and/or domination" (Rodriguez 2017), and since food production is symbolically and intrinsically linked to structures of domination, we find that a consistently anti-oppressive veganism disrupts that in a way that is inherently queer. Plainly stated, LGBTQIA+ people who are not vegan uphold their own oppression.

*Cited Works*

Adams, C. J. (2015). *The Sexual Politics of Meat: A Feminist-Vegetarian Critical Theory*. Bloomsbury Publishing.

Alkon, A. and Mares, T. (2012). Food Sovereignty in US Food Movements: Radical Visions and Neoliberal Constraints. *Springer Science and Business Media*.

Bock, B. and H. Buller (2013). Healthy, Happy and Humane: Evidence in Farm Animal Welfare Policy. *European Society for Rural Sociology*, 53 (3): 390–411.

Chowdhury, S. (2019). *Ethical Consumption Under Capitalism? in* Julia Feliz Brueck (ed), *Veganism of*

*Color: Decentering Whiteness in Human and Nonhuman Liberation*. Sanctuary Publishers.

Cohen, M. (2017). Animal Colonialism: The Case of Milk. *American Journal of International Law Unbound*, 111: 267-271.

Cudworth, E. (2015). Killing Animals: Sociology, Species Relations and Institutionalized Violence. *The Sociological Review*, 63 (1): 1–18.

Deerinwater, J. (2018). Our Pride: Honoring and Recognizing Our Two Spirit Past and Present. *ReWire News*.

Evaristo, B. (2014). The Idea that African Homosexuality Was a Colonial Import is a Myth. *The Guardian*: https://www.theguardian.com/commentisfree/2014/mar/08/african-homosexuality-colonial-import-myth

Feliz Brueck, J. (2019). *Veganism of Color: Decentering Whiteness in Human and Nonhuman Liberation*. Sanctuary Publishers.

Gaard, G. (1997). Toward a Queer Ecofeminism. *Hypatia*, 12 (1): 114–37.

Han, E. and J. O'Mahoney (2014). The British Colonial Origins of Anti-Gay Laws. *The Washington*

*Post*: https://www.washingtonpost.com/
news/monkey-cage/wp/2014/10/30/the-british-
colonial-origins-of-anti-gay-laws

Han, E. and J. O'Mahoney (2018). *How Britain's
Colonial Legacy Still Affects LGBT Politics Around the
World.* The Conversation:
http://theconversation.com/how-britains-colonial-
legacy-still-affects-lgbt-politics-around-the-world-
95799

Holt, D. M. (2008) "Unlikely Allies against Factory
Farms: Animal Rights Advocates and
Environmentalists." *Agriculture and Human Values*,
25 (2): 169–71.

Jiménez Rodríguez, A. (2017). 'Strange Coupling':
Vegan Ecofeminism and Queer Ecologies in Theory
and in Practice CHAPTER 1: A Brief Survey of the
Field of Ecofeminism." *Revista de Lenguas
Modernas*, 25.

Kalende, V. (2014). *Africa: Homophobia is a Legacy
of Colonialism.* The Guardian:
https://www.theguardian.com/world/2014/apr/30/
africa-homophobia-legacy-colonialism

Kolbe, E. (2013). Won't You Be My Neighbor? Living
with Concentrated Animal Feeding Operations. *Iowa
Law Review*: 99.

Kolb-Untinen, N. M. (2018). *The Disruptive Potential of a Queer Vegan Praxis*. University Honors Theses Paper: 618.

Muller, S. M. (2019). Personal communication.

Plumwood, V. (1991) Nature, Self, and Gender: Feminism, Environmental Philosophy, and the Critique of Rationalism. *Hypatia*, 6 (1): 3-27.

Rivera-Rideau, P. R. (2015). *Remixing Reggaeton: The Cultural Politics of Race in Puerto Rico*. Duke University Press.

Simonsen, R. R. (2012). A queer vegan manifesto. *Journal for Critical Animal Studies*, 10(3): 51-81.

The Vegan Society (2019). History: https://www.vegansociety.com/about-us/history

Timmins, B. (2017). Who Were the World's Very Earliest Vegans? *Independent*, UK: https://www.independent.co.uk/life-style/who-were-the-world-s-very-earliest-vegans-a7668831.html

Williams, T. (2019). *Before European Christians Forced Gender Roles, Native Americans Acknowledged 5 Genders*. Bipartisan Report:

https://bipartisanreport.com/2016/06/19/before-european-christians-forced-gender-roles-native-americans-acknowledged-5-genders/

# 2 REFLECTIONS FROM THE LGBTQIA+ VEGAN COMMUNITY:

## INTERCONNECTIONS

FELIZ BRUECK AND McNEILL

## *Climate Catastrophe, Animal Agriculture, and the World's Marginalized Communities*

Chris H.

*If you have come here to help me, you are wasting your time. But if you have come because your liberation is bound up with mine, then let us work together.*

-Aboriginal activist group (1968), "Queensland," Colonized-named "Australia"

A hard fact for us white people to accept is that we've been given a deeply flawed, even violent idea of what "help" means. Until we accept this reality we will keep acting as "white saviors," helping marginalized communities self-servingly rather than moving in true solidarity with them. The reality is that the majority of white people have yet to acknowledge that current global power structures have been designed to treat us, white people, as the definition of "fully human." We, white people, treat ourselves as individuals of "neutral" race even as we "racialize" Black people, Indigenous people, and other People of Color. We, white people, also grant ourselves individual and collective unearned structural advantages compared to "racialized people". This is "white privilege." As white people, whatever the challenges we face, our lives are not systematically harder because we are white.

Truthfully, we live in a bubble of whiteness, where we remain both willfully and unconsciously ignorant about the world which everyone else experiences. Our unearned social advantage, due to our race, insulates us from the trauma, harm, and oppression that holds back other racialized groups under the white supremacist society we live in. This system protects our status under whiteness, and therefore, this same race-based insulation also protects white people who belong to marginalized communities including white people that identify as trans and queer.

This white supremacist system was socially constructed by wealthy European Christians that had landed on Turtle Island in the late 1600s with the aim of denying the freedoms of Christianity to all other races (Williamson 2017). This enforced white supremacist system quickly adopted just about every form of oppression into itself to sustain first colonialism, and subsequently, neo-colonialism in an effort to exert continual control over other nations through the imbalanced relationships that were initially forged under the expansion of whiteness. In 1965, Kwame Nkrumah – prominent African Independence activist, first elected Prime Minister of Gold Coast, and the first President of Ghana – wrote, "The essence of neo-colonialism is that the State which is subject to it is, in theory, independent and has all the outward trappings of international sovereignty. In reality, its economic system, and thus, its political policy is directed from outside." In essence, neo-colonialism masks the continual exploitation of historically colonized nations (primarily in the Global South) by ensuring that white supremacy remains in control as it has been since people from the European continent, *my own people*, landed on the shores of other nations.

As for my own story, I was formally recognized as autistic in my fifth decade of life. I am also disabled. However, to be clear, I'm disabled by chronic illness and not by autism. Society disables me as an autistic person in the way that it normalizes and centers neurotypical needs, re-actions, and ways of being. In this way, white supremacy exploits and "others" disabled people under systemic *ableism*. This ensures that "Claims of unproven disability after mass violence or in marginalized communities, and hints at mental illness, only serve rhetoric about the 'master race.' It is the easiest way to prove that others are inferior (Barbarin 2018)." Adding to my disability and neurodivergence, I always knew I was of a marginalized gender although I didn't have those words in my vocabulary. I knew I was neither a girl nor a boy. Yet, despite these struggles, I acknowledge that I am protected by my whiteness. I also have many other unearned social advantages – privileges – that people placed "lower" in the hierarchy of white supremacy do not enjoy. For example, I am securely housed and employed, higher educated, from a financially secure extended family, from the Global North – specifically, Europe– and human.

I started to vaguely understand what it means to be white and benefit from unearned privileges when I was a young teenager. One of our teachers showed us the first episode of the 1977 mini-series *Roots* during one of our humanities lessons. The series *Roots* follows the experiences and struggles of an African person stolen from their village and enslaved in the United States. This was my first memory of honestly being shown how white European people systematically enslaved Black African people. But even so, beyond watching the series, we were not challenged to take the time to go further to understand how white European people are complicit in the continual harms that have come out of chattel enslavement and European colonial violence. My humanities courses at school did, however, start to make me aware of interconnected issues around white capitalism. For example, I learned a little about how we, white Europeans, have violently impoverished the Global South as well as the majority of Black People, Indigenous People, and other People of Color living in the Global North as well. I also learned how multinational, white-dominated corporations use white capitalism to continue the violent legacy of white colonialism. Fundamentally, the creation and expansion of white supremacy was integral to white European colonizers plundering the rest of the world. We used deceit, theft of land and resources on a global scale, enslavement, and genocide to get what we wanted. Another tool of colonialism and oppression which we used was to bring "domesticated" nonhumans animals to stolen Indigenous lands. We destroyed Indigenous societies through genocide while breeding our farmed animals in huge numbers and enforced European industrialized animal agriculture in place of Indigenous foodways.

Faced with these truths, it became difficult for me to ignore the grim realities of industrial animal farming. Eventually, it became impossible to look back once I found a "Carbon Footprint Calculator" that included food. I filled it in carefully and was shocked at the end of the calculation upon learning that choosing to eat foods taken from animals, including meat, eggs, and dairy, was the largest way that I was creating greenhouse gas emissions daily. At the time, hardly anyone, even those who saw themselves as "white green people," were sharing the fact that our biggest impacts came from daily choices we made at least three meals a day. I learned that our farming of animals accounts for around half of all food-related greenhouse gas emissions, which are far out of proportion with the calories we get from "food animals" (Gerber et al. 2013). The more I read about this topic, the more I learned how our industrial farming of animals is intrinsically tied to climate change, and I realized that in order to become truly sustainable, we would need to have awareness of the sources of the foods we ate and their hidden, true costs.

As a result, I became vegan.

## Meeting White Veganism

When I went away to university to study physics – which I believed would help me understand the deep truths of the universe – I began to intentionally eat plant-based food. Eventually, I did the research to prove I could eat a healthy, balanced vegan diet and fully committed to being vegan. When my physics funding dried up, I turned my scientific training towards understanding human nutrition, plant agriculture, climate science, and related areas.

When I first found the vegan movement, I felt like I had found a community of like-minded people; it was difficult to ignore, however, that I found myself part of a circle of almost exclusively white vegans. Eventually, I realized that the white vegan movement was and is very happy to be considered a social justice movement while refusing to listen to other social justice movements. Truthfully, we white vegans take advantage of our white privilege to silence and disregard marginalized people by insisting on drawing a line between the "one" true community that truly needs our "help" (specifically, nonhumans) without taking into account the varying interconnections between the oppression of nonhumans and humans. This type of single-issue veganism is commonly referred to as "white veganism," in which we, white people, try to mask our "white saviorism" by insisting we are just trying to "help" a specific exploited community over all other communities exploited under the very system designed to benefit us as human *and* white. Rather than dismantling any form of oppression, we white vegans merely uphold it and benefit from it.

I learned all this thanks to the labor of Black vegans, starting with Dr. A. Breeze Harper of Sistah Vegan, Kevin Tillman of the vegan hip-hop movement, and Aph Ko and Syl Ko of Aphro-ism. From these Black vegans, I learned to talk and write less so that I can read and listen more. Thus, I could learn far more from those who are systematically silenced in the vegan movement: Black vegans, Indigenous vegans, other Vegans of Color, and non-human beings.

I learned that we white people who are vegan both uphold and gain huge unearned benefits from the exact oppressive supremacist system that we claim to be dismantling. We are never the target of racism, have greater access to financial resources, and are treated as though we were intellectually, ethically, aesthetically, and, in all ways, "superior" humans by other white people. These unearned benefits apply just as much within white veganism as in our wider white dominated society. Frankly, the oppression of non-human beings, our white privilege, and the global oppression of marginalized humans are all aspects of white supremacy. I also learned that, no matter my good intentions, I was reproducing the violence of white supremacy and harming Black people, Indigenous people, People of Color in vegan and non-vegan spaces.

Vegans of Color called me out to learn better and do better. So, I enrolled in anti-racism courses and made a commitment to actively work against whiteness. Thus, I finally acknowledged that the white-centered vegan movement's problem goes far beyond white saviorism. The horrible fact, which I learned from my Black and Indigenous anti-racism teachers, is that we, white vegans, are every bit as racist as are white nonvegans. As Feliz-Brueck boldly stated in their book, *Veganism of Color* (2019), "White veganism *is* white supremacy." Centered on the most privileged group, white veganism is merely an extension of the supremacist system that marginalizes every being on this Planet.

As white vegans, we use and exploit nonhuman animals as a way to exploit and attack Black people, Indigenous people, and other People of Color. Whether willfully, or unconsciously, we specifically uphold white supremacy by treating racism and other forms of oppression of humans as "solved" or secondary problems – "for the animals." As Julia Feliz Brueck writes in *Veganism in an Oppressive World: A Vegans-of-Color Community Project* (2017), "[A]s we [Vegans of Color] fight for nonhuman animal rights... we also have to fight for our own rights in a world based on white supremacy and systemic oppression." The author further explained (Feliz Brueck 2018):

> *In our world, the accepted way to be is human.*
>
> *Human is the "norm" and standard that is applied across the world through a supremacist hierarchy that places different species on different levels. We all know this in basic terms as speciesism, where humans are at the top and nonhumans are seen as "less than."*
>
> *For centuries, this is also what has been done to marginalized humans through a hierarchy based on skin colors, for example, in which anti-blackness is reinforced and applied throughout the world. To be Black and Brown is to be seen as "less than" because that is what is taught in our society subconsciously. These issues have not been solved and are still very much present in society today — right now.*
>
> *And the thing is that this type of hierarchy follows Vegans of Color even in vegan spaces. We can't just leave our skin color at*

*the door and unless you are aware of how we experience our lives — the microaggressions, the racism, the xenophobia, the stereotypes... you might unintentionally add to it.*

*This happens quite often when we are told to give up our safety and march side-by-side racists and xenophobes "for the animals." Or when we are expected to show up to protest with police presence at an event even though People of Color are targeted by police for just being Brown and Black. Or when we are told that "human oppression is not as important as nonhuman animal oppression" or when well-known "leaders" in the movement preach for the tolerance of bigots and bigotry "for the animals."*

The reality is that white supremacy has subsumed almost every form of oppression into one violent, self-sustaining system. This means that the whiteness of white veganism upholds the oppression of human communities. Both white vegans and white nonvegans alike are stuck in a false "good-bad" binary: we all want to believe we are "good people." We want to believe that we are "good white people" who are "not racist." However, we refuse to own the fact white supremacy is a system that no white person can "opt out" from. Therefore, all white people are racist. By refusing to evolve beyond this binary and call ourselves what we are, we continue to harm racialized people including those that walk with us for other marginalized communities despite the dangers that we put them through with our lack of awareness of how life operates for others under racism. Yet, to insist on the idea that only "bad people" are racist is to further attach ourselves to white supremacy in a time where anti-racism work is an option open to anyone willing to face our reality as white people. As scholar and activist Ijeoma Oluo (2020) writes, "The beauty of anti-racism is that you don't have to pretend to be free of racism to be an anti-racist. Anti-racism is the commitment to fight racism wherever you find it, including in yourself. And it's the only way forward." Racism continues to give white supremacy fuel to persist, and only through anti-racism work will we, white people, be finally able to begin to rid racialized people from the normalized oppression that our ancestors forced on them.

However, it must be noted that anti-racism work alone is not enough to undo the harm of white supremacy since the oppression of nonhuman

animals is both another form of white supremacy
and a tool used to oppress these very humans.

## Animalization Under White Supremacy
## and Climate Chaos

Our oppression of nonhuman animals is deeply
tied to the reasons why we are now dealing with a
climate crisis. The UN Environment Project has
affirmed that the Global North's taste for diets rich
in "meat and dairy products" are environmentally
unsustainable (Hertwich 2010). There is not enough
fertile land and fresh water for the vast numbers of
animals we would need to exploit if 7 or 10 billion
people all ate that way.  The greenhouse gases and
industrial quantities of wastes from artificially
breeding so many animals could not be mitigated
safely. While the Global North is largely responsible
for the impending climate catastrophe, climate
chaos pits marginalized communities around the
globe against each other for the benefit of the
Global North over the Global South. The white-
dominated countries that have the most economic
power – such as the U.S.A., Canada, Russia, U.K.,
and the rest of white Europe as well as Australia and
New Zealand – "the Global North," actively try to
hide our destructive actions by "victim blaming"
countries that are still impoverished due to white

European colonialism and neo-colonialism. These countries – such as Nigeria, Ethiopia, Egypt, Kenya, India, Haiti, Bolivia, Palestine, and Vietnam to name just a few – are known as "the Global South."

To further understand all these inter-connections and imbalances under climate catastrophe, we must start with the process of animalization in the context of white supremacy. In their book, *Aphro-ism: Essays on Pop Culture, Feminism, and Black Veganism from Two Sisters* (2017), Aph Ko and Syl Ko explain that animalization is a key process in white supremacy. Syl Ko writes, "When we refer to a person or a group as 'animalistic'... What we are saying is *they don't behave or look or believe properly*, where what is 'proper' is defined by Eurocentric, white ideals. In other words, they *deviate from whiteness*." Once groups have been "animalized" this enables "coloniality." As Nelson Maldonado-Torres (2007) writes, the "long-standing patterns of power that emerged as a result of colonialism, but that define culture, labor, intersubjective relations, and knowledge production well beyond the strict limits of colonial administrations." This has been the case for hundreds of years.

I recognize that my white Christian European ancestors industrialized animalization. That is to say, white capitalism created the whole industrial complex founded upon white supremacy. Capitalism weaponized white supremacy against Black people, Indigenous people, other People of Color, women and other people of marginalized gender, disabled people, neurodivergent people, queer people, and people at any and all these and other intersections of oppression. Once white European people had established this social system based on domination and power over "animalized" groups, we used it to build white capitalism, specifically within colonized countries. We industrialized exploitation, in the genocide of Indigenous peoples, and the mass killing and enslavement of Black African people, and the inter-generational terrorization of Black people through rape, forced pregnancy, forced wet nursing of white babies, and enslavement of Black children, and the theft of Indigenous land and resources in areas of the Global North including Turtle Island, the U.S. We also industrialized the abuse of nonhumans, especially in farming. To this very hour, we, white people, are taught to "dehumanize" and "animalize" every living being who isn't admitted into the tiny category of *white people*.

Julia Feliz Brueck (2018) emphasizes, "[S]ingle-issue veganism, which has become the mainstream "norm," is lacking in the awareness of animalization as a tool of white supremacy and how it gave rise to an offshoot of speciesism, *racialized speciesism*, that affects People of Color specifically." Therefore, ignoring the connections between race, colonialism, nonhuman exploitation, and climate catastrophe means that single-issue white environmentalism and single-issue climate change activism have exactly the same fundamental flaws as white veganism. In fact, the current climate emergency is far from being "only an environmental issue." Climate catastrophe is a social justice issue, which has arisen during an era of white-dominated industrial capitalism that depends on animalization and white supremacy. This global interlocking system of oppressions is fundamental to white capitalism and neo-colonial global control. Extreme exploitation and impoverishment of humans, nonhumans, the biosphere, and mineral resources are key market features, not "market failures." Therefore, to slow and reverse climate change, we must dismantle the whole white supremacist and neo-colonial system. Climate catastrophe is, in reality, an economic, political, neo-colonial, social justice, human rights life-and-death issue, and in conjunction with the exploitation of non-human animals, it's one more of the many ways white supremacy harms and kills marginalized people.

## Climate Catastrophe and the Effects
## on Marginalized Communities

Our white supremacist capitalist system intentionally and systematically impoverishes people. The most impoverished people are the most likely to live in fragile housing in disaster-prone areas (The World Bank 2016). They are the most likely to work in the sectors at high risk extreme weather events such as agriculture and fishing. Oppressed groups of people also receive far less government and community support to recover after disasters. Injustice make "natural disasters" such as storms, floods, droughts, and earthquakes far more damaging. Adding to this, existing social injustices are always exacerbated by any crisis (Goodfellow 2015). That is because marginalized and impoverished people have fewer resources they can use to reduce the damage and repair afterwards. For example, women and girls are more likely to die during catastrophic climate events than are men and boys (Cannon 2002, Doocy 2013).

In addition, Black people, Indigenous people, other People of Color, disabled people, all marginalized people are also disproportionately harmed by climate change due to their social disadvantages. Adding to this, it's important to recognize that Black people, Indigenous people, and other People of Color make up the *majority* of people that identify as LGBTQIA+. Thus, Black people, Indigenous people, and other People of Color from both the Global North and South are harmed *the most* by climate change. Meanwhile, white people dominate and distort the global debate about the climate crisis, which is directly linked to resource hoarding and resource over-consumption.

Within the Global South, people are already facing some of the worst effects of climate change (Wildman et al. 1996). It's important to note that the emissions from smallholder farms in the Global South are in no way equivalent to those of indus-trialized farms in the Global North (Vermeulen and Wollenberg 2007). There are millions of smallholder farmers in the Global South (each with less than 2 hectares of land) which are directly feeding and supporting farming communities. All these smallholder farms together only cause about one third of global farming greenhouse gas (GHG) emissions (FAO 2014). In contrast, industrial farms in the Global North often produce less food per hectare (Steinfeld 2006) than properly supported smallholder farms. Therefore, when we talk about cutting GHG emissions from our farming, we must recognize the disproportionate harm caused *by* our large industrial farms in the Global North (Althor et al. 2016, Walker 2012). Sadly, the list of climate disasters that have begun to affect the Global South is already long: critical resource scarcity in Nigeria, Uganda, Ethiopia, and Sudan; rising sea levels threatening Kiribati, Maldives, the Marshall Islands, and Tuvalu; thousands dead in flooding in Venezuela, Bangladesh, and Pakistan; thousands dead in hurricanes in Mozambique and Bangladesh; and death and devastation caused by huge fires in the Amazon and the Congo Basin to name just a few.

Specifically, within the Global North itself, we find that environmental racism is rife in white-dominated industrialized countries like the USA (Walker 2012, Goodfellow 2015) and in unison with climate catastrophe, which means that Black, Brown, and Indigenous People of Color are and will face the worst effects even in countries with the most economic power due to the racialized social disparities (Chapman 2015). Examples of this include when Hurricane Katrina hit New Orleans, about 70% of city residents were Black. George Bush's delayed response to that crisis was anti-Black racism, a founding principle of the white colonial USA (Goodfellow 2015). Another more recent example, Puerto Rico, a USA colonial territory, is still waiting for more than half of the billions in USA federal funds promised two years after Hurricanes

Irma and Maria hit the island in 2017. It is estimated that about 5,000 Puerto Ricans died after Hurricane Maria due to the USA government's slow and inadequate response.

Last but not least, nonhuman animals are also profoundly harmed by climate catastrophe and environmental degradation and have been. In 2020, Australia experienced the worst fires in its modern history. WWF-Australia (O'Gorman 2020) estimates that around 1.25 billion free-living animals died due to the fires. However, this is comparable to the number of animals killed for food every few days – estimates including fish range from around 0.5 to 3 billion per day (The Vegan Calculator 2020, Sentient Media 2020). Climate change is also already causing animals and other species to become extinct. One recent estimate (Román-Palacios and Wiens 2020) is that at least half of species may not be able to disperse quickly enough to avoid extinction due to changes in climate, particularly due to rapid increases in maximum temperatures. Even though some species may be able to adapt to changing conditions, there could be up to 30% extinction rates of animals and other species by 2070.

## Veganism and Its Environmental Impact

Research shows that transitioning away from reliance upon industrial farming of animals toward plant-based ways of living can reduce our harmful impact on the environment. We must ensure that smallholder farmers in the Global South are properly supported so they can in turn support their whole communities. This would bring huge environmental and health benefits to people living in the Global South. However, in the Global North, those of us who can freely choose plant-based living can individually as well as collectively achieve huge environmental and health benefits. If we collectively transition toward more plant-based methods and diets, we could reduce food-related GHG emissions by 29% – 70% by 2050 compared with a reference scenario (Marco et al. 2016).

Major global organizations have also affirmed the research and that one effective way for us as individuals to help slow the climate crisis is by improving our diets. Specifically, the International Panel on Climate Change (IPCC) has advocated that we reduce our reliance on farming animals to slow climate change. In 2019, a leaked IPCC report stated, "The consumption of healthy and sustainable diets, such as those based on coarse grains, pulses and vegetables, and nuts and seeds…

presents major opportunities for reducing greenhouse gas emissions (Mckie 2019)." In addition, a 2018 study confirmed this when researchers looked at the full environmental impacts of almost 40,000 farms in 119 countries and 90% of all foods that are eaten. From "farm to fork" – in terms of land use, GHG emissions, fresh water use and air and water pollution – the study found that a completely plant-based diet is probably the single biggest step we can take as individuals to reduce the harm we do to the planet (Carrington 2018).

## Systemic-Wide Change

Devastating changes to our world are already happening. Why is the Global North still failing to act decisively to end the climate emergency? Because privileged people in the Global North are disproportionately causing the harm *yet* are protected from the consequences. The harm and oppression of marginalized people – Black people, Indigenous people, other People of Color, women and other people of marginalized gender, disabled people, neurodivergent people, LGBTIQA+ people, and people at any and all these and other intersections will continue to worsen until we dismantle white capitalism, white supremacy, and white neo-colonial governments. We must move beyond white saviorism and our shallow understanding of cosmetic "helping." Instead, we must work collectively towards consistent and urgent, rapid transformation if we are to create radical change and liberation.

We do not have any more time for in-consistency or single-issue advocacy. We cannot solve climate catastrophe without addressing all manifestations of white supremacy, including industrial animal agriculture. We cannot fully address the impacts of industrial animal agriculture whilst we freely continue to support it. We must collectively bring about a new, just system. Meanwhile, we need to make the best individual choices we can under oppression and influence others to do likewise.

We white people urgently need to embrace anti-racist veganism as part of our collective liberation, which must include bringing an end to the climate emergency. We either make a commitment to do consistent anti-oppression work, or we are complicit in the intersectional crisis. We either learn how to follow in humility and true solidarity, or we will keep on reproducing the violence of white supremacy. We must make reparations, pay our teachers, and focus on dismantling our individual and collective white supremacy. We white people all need to get and stay on our authentic anti-racism and consistent anti-oppression journey every day for the rest of our lives.

*Cited Works*

Aboriginal Activist Group (1968) *If You Have Come to Help Me*: http://northlandposter.com/if-you-have-come-to-help-me

Althor, G., Watson, J. E. M. and Fuller, R. A. (2016) Global mismatch between greenhouse gas emissions and the burden of climate change. *Scientific Reports,* 6 (20281).

Barbarin, I. (2018) *Ableism Is the Go-To Disguise for White Supremacy. Too Many People Are Falling for It*. Rewire News: https://rewire.news/article/2018/11/19/ableism-is-the-go-to-disguise-for-white-supremacy-too-many-people-are-falling-for-it

Cannon, T. (2002) Gender and Climate Hazards in Bangladesh. *Gender and Development*, 10 (2), Climate Change: 45-50.

Carrington, D. (2018) Avoiding meat and dairy is 'single biggest way' to reduce your impact on Earth. *The Guardian.*

Chapman, S. (2015) Environmental Justice, Climate Change, & Racial Justice. *PDE Climate Change Outreach Roundtable.*

Doocy, S., Dick, A., Daniels, A., and Kirsch, T.D. (2013) The Human Impact of Tropical Cyclones: A Historical Review of Events 1980-2009 and Systematic Literature Review. *PLOS Currents Disasters.* Edition 1.

FAO (2014) Family Farmers Feeding the world, Caring for the Earth, *FAO, Rome.*

Feliz Brueck, J. (2017) *Veganism in an Oppressive World: A Vegans-of-Color Community Project.* Sanctuary Publishers.

Feliz Brueck, J. (2018) *An Intro to Consistent Anti-Oppression Veganism*, Vegans of Color Mini Conference, Dublin, Ireland: https://medium.com/@jd.feliz/an-intro-to-consistent-anti-oppression-veganism

Feliz Brueck, J. (2019) *Veganism of Color: Decentering Whiteness in Nonhuman and Human Liberation.* Sanctuary Publishers.

Gerber, P.J., Steinfeld, H., Henderson, B., Mottet, A., Opio, C., Dijkman, J., Falcucci, A., and Tempio, G. (2013) Tackling Climate Change Through Livestock – A global assessment of emissions and mitigation opportunities. Rome, Italy: Food and Agriculture Organization of the United Nations (FAO).

Goodfellow, M. (2015) Climate Change Is Easier to Ignore because Right Now It's People of Colour Who Suffer the Most. *Media Diversified*: https://mediadiversified.org/2015/03/19/climate-change-is-easier-to-ignore-because-right-now-its-people-of-colour-who-suffer-the-most

Ko, A. and Ko, S. (2017) *Aphro-ism: Essays on Pop Culture, Feminism, and Black Veganism from Two Sisters*. Lantern Books.

Maldonado-Torres, N. (2007) *On the Coloniality of Being*. Cultural Studies, 21 (2): 240 – 270.

Marco, S., Godfray, H.C.J., Rayner, M. and Scarborough, P. (2016) Analysis and valuation of the health and climate change co-benefits of dietary change. *PNAS*, 113 (15): 4146-4151.

McKie, R., (2019) We must change food production to save the world, says leaked report. *The Guardian*.

Nkrumah, Kwame (1965) *Neo-Colonialism, The Last Stage of Imperialism.* Thomas Nelson & Sons, Ltd., London: https://www.marxists.org/subject/africa/nkrumah/neo-colonialism/introduction.htm

O'Gorman, D. (2020). *Statement from WWF-Australia on Australia's bushfire emergency.* WWF.

Oluo, I. (2020) Twitter: https://twitter.com/ijeomaoluo/status/1150565193832943617

Román-Palacios, C. and Wiens, J. J. (2020) Recent responses to climate change reveal the drivers of species extinction and survival. *Proc Natl Acad Sci USA.*

Sentient Media (2020) *How Many Animals Killed for Our Food Every Minute*: https://sentientmedia.org/how-many-animals-are-killed-for-food-every-day

Steinfeld et al. (2006) *Livestock's Long Shadow: Environmental Issues and Options.* FAO, Rome: http://www.fao.org/3/a0701e/a0701e00.htm

The Vegan Calculator (2020): https://thevegancalculator.com/animal-slaughter

The World Bank (2016) *Breaking the Link Between Extreme Weather and Extreme Poverty*: https://www.worldbank.org/en/news/feature/2016/11/14/breaking-the-link-between-extreme-weather-and-extreme-poverty

UN IPCC Special Report (2019) Climate Change and Land. IPCC: https://www.ipcc.ch/srccl

Vermeulen, S. and Wollenberg, E. (2017). CCAFS Info Note: A rough estimate of the proportion of global emissions from agriculture due to smallholders. *CCAFS*: https://ccafs.cgiar.org/publications/rough-estimate-proportion-global-emissions-agriculture-due-smallholders

Walker, G., (2012) Environmental justice: concepts evidence and politics. *Routledge, London.*

Wildman, S. M. (1996) Privilege Revealed: How Invisible Preference Undermines America. *NYU Press:* 87.

Williamson, V. (2017) *When White Supremacy Came to Virginia.* The Brookings Institution: https://www.brookings.edu/blog/fixgov/2017/08/15/when-white-supremacy-came-to-virginia

## *Oppressive Dichotomies: Fighting for Animals with Queer Liberation*

Moe Constantine

As a teenager and young adult struggling with my gender identity, I was, in the back of my mind, concerned with how my exhausting battle to gain access to my own gender was distracting me from more important issues. Being queer felt like, at the time, a distraction from my true calling as an animal liberation activist. Until my first year of graduate school, my goal was to assimilate into cisgender society as quickly as possible. During this time, in a course on critical race theory, I read a chapter from the 1979 book *White Hero Black Beast: Racism, Sexism, and the Mask of Masculinity*, in which Paul Hoch wrote "the virility of the nation is validated by its conquest over the local beasts" (p. 57). He continued on to describe examples of this, recounting how (in terms of white civilization) "the Roman Empire was forged in a contest against the barbarians; the nineteenth century European empires in one against the restless natives of Africa; and that of the young American nation against the indian savages" (p. 57). The "barbarians" that must be conquered in each of these cases were the Indigenous populations who had yet to be "liberated" from nature and were, therefore, "uncivilized." This made me recognize that while the white male is held as the epitome of the civilized person, opposing qualities like blackness, femininity, and animality are externalized and "othered." Those embodying characteristics outside of white, male, and human are relegated to the bottom of the moral hierarchy while the latter was and is still placed at the top.

In white society, these "others" must be tightly controlled for fear that their moral corruptness and barbaric ways will permeate through society. From here arises the prolific white savior narrative that underlies much of Western identity where the white male must save the white female from the darker, bestial forces. In essence, the use of the male/female binary and human/animal binary, sexism, cisgenderism, and speciesism are all mobilized in the construction of this racist narrative that continues to excuse the violence committed against all that are not white men.

That the moral hierarchy of white civilization is rooted in the human/animal dichotomy has had a number of consequences for racialized and gendered people. It has tied the fates of racial, gender, queer, and animal justice. It means that, to be invested in speciesist beliefs and actions, requires an investment in racist, misogynist, heterosexist, cisgenderist dichotomies that enable the creation of an amoral or immoral "other" that can occupy the bottom rungs of the moral hierarchy. It also means that the white masculinity of Western civilization can be challenged not only with anti-racist work or feminism but with all that it claims it is not: blackness, indigeneity, femininity, queerness, and animality. Any display of such characteristics represents a deviation from the norm and has been taught to be feared by white society. In this way, fighting for queer liberation is a part of fighting for animal liberation and vice versa. In essence, I came to realize that being transgender is not a distraction from my work as an animal liberationist but rather a part of it.

Like queer people, animal liberation activists face great resistance from society because their assertion of our kinship with nonhumans challenges the carefully constructed dichotomies that justify society's manner of existence. Animal liberation activists are labeled as terrorists and imprisoned for their daring to challenge our speciesist views toward other animals. It is important to acknowledge the interlocking oppressions of racialized people, women and queers, and nonhuman animals and seek collective freedom. Many that do understand speciesism as a foundational oppressive paradigm still do not acknowledge the consequences that speciesism has on marginalized human groups as well. For example, a somewhat common method used by the animal liberation movement to gain the sympathies of the public is to compare the oppression of Black people to the oppression of nonhuman animals. Animal liberation groups will put up billboards and posters with a depiction of African slavery in the Americas next to an image from the inside of a factory farm to show the similarities between the enslavement of Africans in the 17th, 18th, and 19th centuries and the current enslavement of farmed animals. They present this comparison as though the enslavement of Black, Brown, and Indigenous people is something of the past, something we have overcome, and can now follow suit for our treatment of other animals. Yet a quick look at the prison industry and the food industry will dispel this illusion.

The animal liberation activists also present this comparison as original when, in fact, it is as old as civilization and has been used over and over to subjugate both racialized people and nonhuman animals. This comparison was used to *promote* slavery, and yet now an assumption has been made that this same comparison, in the same white society, can be used to *reject* slavery. But the moral hierarchy which places both Blackness and animality at the bottom has not gone away: it still provides essential support for the maintenance of white society, and so it seems unlikely that this comparison could be used to combat speciesist ideas. Julia Feliz Brueck explains this well, using the term "racialized speciesism" to describe how the "speciesism experienced by People of Color [is] upheld through white supremacy and the use of nonhuman animals as a tool to establish these hierarchies of inequality and oppression" (2018, para. 6). In "Intersectionality in Mi'kmaw and Settler Vegan Values," Margaret Robinson discusses the protesting by white vegans of the annual Indigenous hunt that happens in the Niagara region of Canada and how, as a result, "Indigenous communities tend to view the animal rights activism by Settlers as part of the ongoing genocide of Indigenous cultures and people...In this way, the oppression of Indigenous people is part of a larger pattern of domination that includes oppressions such as speciesism" (2017, p. 74). What they are explaining is that to effectively advocate for animals, animal activists must acknowledge that speciesism is a tool used to oppress all "others," not just nonhumans. In these examples of the billboard comparisons and Indigenous hunt protests, the animal liberation movement, which should pose a threat to white civilization, ends up instead borrowing its weapons.

White civilization also depends on the male/female binary, so just as with the human/animal binary, to step outside of it or to claim that it does not exist at all is to challenge the structure of white society and risk its reproduction. The gay liberation movement in the United States, for example, was strongly opposed by the U.S. government because of the challenge it posed. However, by making its primary goal the recognition of monogamous, same-sex marriages, the movement was able to carve itself a spot in white society and call itself a success. The gay liberation movement achieved their "liberation" through their assimilation. Both the comparison of farmed animals with African slavery and the fight for marriage equality profess to further the cause of liberating a marginalized group but simultaneously forget to examine the underlying cause of their marginalization. This was true in my own journey, in which I forgot, or never understood, the underlying system of oppression, which led me to believe that being queer was not relevant to being anti-speciesist.

When I started hormone replacement therapy, I felt like I had finally been given access to my own gender. For the first time, other people would see me how I wanted to be seen — as a normal, cisgender (white) man. However, after reading Hoch's chapter, I had to ask myself how my refusal to step outside the boundaries of white masculinity (whether in an effort to "pass" or not) reflected my investment in maintaining white society, which can only be understood in terms of what it is not, what it has "othered." As a transgender man, I am familiar with how shame is used as a weapon, justified by society's moral hierarchy, yet like many others who are white and masculine, I have the ability to remedy my exclusion by accepting the terms of society. But doing so is not only detrimental to other trans people, it also makes me complicit in the harm inflicted upon other 'others,' like nonhuman animals. As I have learned throughout my life, while institutions and systems make it easy to uphold discriminatory beliefs and practices, these practices are replicated in every social interaction and by each individual who does not challenge them.

Is it my responsibility, as an animal liberation activist, to come out as transgender? This is a very personal question and cannot be answered objectively. For me personally, being openly transgender and refusing to assimilate into white male society has become a source of strength for my animal liberation activism. I want to use my gender expression to help dismantle the pillars that uphold racism, sexism, and speciesism, like my transgender siblings did before me. Our belief that humans are not a part of nature and that we uniquely have intrinsic value among all other living and nonliving beings is just as outrageous as our belief that humans can be consigned to two categories of expression. In fact, these beliefs arise from the same underlying belief system, one that is carefully designed and maintained to benefit only a very few beings on this earth. To challenge it and do my best work as an animal liberation activist, I must step outside of this worldview, its oppressive dichotomies, and resist assimilation.

*Cited Works*

Feliz Brueck, J. (2018). Racialized speciesism? *Medium*. Retrieved from: www.medium.com/@jd.feliz/racialized-speciesism-991eb3653ba0

Feliz Brueck, J. (Ed). (2017). *Veganism in an oppressive world: A vegans of color community project*. Sanctuary Publishers.

Hoch, P. (1979). "Masculinity as interracial competition for women?" In *White hero black beast: Racism, sexism, and the mask of masculinity*. London: Pluto Press.

## *It's Not Because I'm Vegan*

Brooke Shephard

I choose to identify by two labels: vegan and asexual.

Veganism was an easy jump for my partner. Asexuality took a bit of an adjustment period.
As an activist, I am open with my veganism, prepared for any argument. As an asexual, only my partner knows, and we are happy.

The two labels had never intersected before until 2019.

I finally felt heard – understood – by someone whose work I had stumbled on. The person was vegan, had been in a long-term relationship, and was openly asexual.

However, the year 2019 seemed full of ex-vegans, and in one neatly scripted video on why they needed to go back to exploiting nonhuman animals, this same person suddenly erased both of my identities. Their ex-vegan video consisted of a long-winded explanation of their reasons.

I, and most vegans, had heard all of them before, every single one was an unnecessary death sentence for nonhuman animals rooted in untruths ("veganism is unsustainable") or passing off accountability of the choices we can and should make ("not everyone can be vegan;" "I can still love animals and eat them too").

One, however, hit me especially hard.

They divulged that they now knew that they had never really been asexual. They claimed that eating plant-based had made them that way, and now that they were eating animals again, they couldn't get enough sex.

Animal exploitation giveth a sex drive, apparently.

My sexuality was erased. My ethics were to blame. Just like getting a cold, veganism was, of course, the cause.

The comments section of the video was full of praise. Other people were happy that this person had seen the light and was now able to enjoy their body the way they were **supposed to**.

I cried.

I cried like I hadn't cried since I told my partner about being asexual.

I cried for myself and for the nonhuman animals that were being used to "fix" something that was not broken.

I don't really think about sex, don't actively desire it outside of a few times a month with my long-term partner. I crave intimacy through cuddling, deep conversation, quality time together. It is different than how most people think, but I am not broken.

Eating the bodies of nonhuman animals will not fix me just like having more sex won't either. Because asexuality is not something to be fixed. For this person, it was simply just another way of justifying the oppression and exploitation of others.

\*\*\*

I feel that my story is tame compared to most people in the LGBTQ+ and vegan community, but we cannot compare our hurt with other people's hurt. Every pain or injustice felt should not be minimized by anyone, including yourself.

My world was changed. I had never had to connect my two labels.

I had never understood what it felt like to have a part of my identity erased.

Veganism has not caused my asexuality, and my asexuality will never stop my veganism. I still choose to keep my asexuality private and my animal activism public, but today and every day, I choose to be a proud asexual vegan.

I am not erased. You are not erased. We are here, and we are valid. These two communities can, should, and will work together.

We need to stop fighting oppression with more oppression. The only way to move forward and to grow the cause in both communities is with acceptance and open-mindedness:

To the LGBTQ+ community: stop marginalizing orientations different from your own and understand that "love is love" should apply to all beings, not just humans.

To the vegan community: create safe spaces for other oppressed groups. Show them the same kindness and compassion we are trying to show nonhuman animals. We can fight for more than one cause.

To both communities: Educate. Educate your-selves and the public so misinformation, like veganism causing asexuality, will not spread and hurt more people.

Speak up for yourself. Speak out for others. Attend marches. Greet those harboring hatred or ignorance with kindness and information. Lend your support to all — those like you and those different from you.

FELIZ BRUECK AND McNEILL

## *A Hierarchy That Should Not Exist*

R.S.

If you've been a victim, be it a victim of societal oppression or something much worse that's hard to put into words, read on.

When I think of oppression, I think about the scary moments when we aren't able to raise a voice, and no one else does it for us or someone else in need either. Being LGBTQIA+ can be one of those journeys. As an innocent child, being different creates a world of its own: the development of triggers and fears, insecurities, negativities, guilt, self-hatred, and so much more. Later in life, lying and the self-hatred becomes a reflex, leaves a scar, and shapes your entire future.

YouTuber Dan Howell, who came out as gay in 2019, said he still faces "existential fear" of being gay. His statement gave me goosebumps because it's so relatable to my own life. This feeling of fear that's stuck deep down in most of us is inexplicable. Regardless of how different our journeys have been, we have that one thing in common, and at least in this day and age, when we can build community from within a virtual platform, we have each other's support and voices.

This experience, although devastating to each of us, is relatable and can make us sympathetic to one another and the experiences of other marginalized humans. Yet, when talking about "support and voices," what about those beings, nonhuman animals, who are unable to garner support through their own voices?

Have we ever questioned the difference between humans and nonhuman animals or even between dogs and pigs? Somehow for us, culture, traditions, tastes, and religion have all outdone our conscience towards the other living beings that also share our planet with us. Dictionary.com provides us with a simplified description of speciesism, which states that it is "discrimination in favor of one species, usually the human species, over another, especially in the exploitation or mistreatment of animals by humans."

As a gay man, how do I see this oppression similar to mine?

Let's imagine a straight person saying, "Our religion, culture, traditions, and history have all been against being queer. It is a disease. We know what is right, and we don't need to justify why we are right. Go and change yourself. We're not - phobic of you, it's just our personal choice." Through this exchange, we can clearly see that a heterosexual person formulates the rejection of someone based on a hierarchy where those with power have the final say over those who have been determined as being "less than."

We can see the same hierarchy when a non-vegan justifies nonhuman animal exploitation within our society by proclaiming, "Our religion, culture, traditions, and history have all been supportive of eating animals. They're meant to be eaten. It is our personal choice. Go and become vegans, but we know we're right."

FELIZ BRUECK AND McNEILL

## *Love Isn't Scarce*

Jocelyn Ramírez

I hesitated to write this piece because it is difficult to write about the truth that you are still discovering, shaping, and naming. Previously, I have written openly about my love for nonhuman animals from the time when I was four years old, and I reflected on the pain that I felt as a child, a heavy type of pain filled with the truth of nonhuman animal exploitation in the world. At that age, I was sensitive to the messages that I received from adults, other children, and the media. These were messages about the planet changing for the worse and non-human animals facing endangerment and extinction; there were also messages about sex, gender, relationships, and love. At four years old, I didn't see anything wrong with my love and attraction for other girls and women. You see, my first crush wasn't horses or pandas, or even that boy named K.[1], but it was B. She was kind and pretty, and my first best friend. To this day, I can remember the joy I felt when she was near me, when we played, and when we talked, but eventually, she

---

[1]Initials for names used to protect the identities and privacy of individuals mentioned

moved. After B. came a line of boys – and I can definitely say they were not like B. Nothing like her. At all. Then came J. Now, J. was also definitely not like B. She was what some might call a tomboy, a great soccer player who didn't take shit from any boys – who truly respected her, but she was also kind and pretty (like really pretty) and my best friend. Eventually, we stopped being friends because she was pretty and sporty, and I was neither.

After J. came more boys (like a lot) and more girls, but I always kept my attraction towards girls a secret. At my school and in my family, no one talked to me or anyone about sex, gender, bodies, dating, or even the concept of attraction(s). The first time I learned about menstruation was actually from J. about how instead of getting pregnant, you just start bleeding once a month. (Believe me, at eight years old that reality scared the shit out of me). Also, the first time I learned about sex was mainly from watching rich, cis straight white people on TV having sex when I was four. Everything outside of that was bad and shameful. All the representation of relationships were of sexually and romantically-involved women – beautiful and successful – that equated to white or very light-skinned, thin, tall, happy, who most importantly, were perfectly in love with a man who was just as white, thin, and tall.

Nothing else represented this ideal for me more than my Barbie dolls. The thing is, I didn't love Barbie – I *loved* Barbie. But I also didn't just love Barbie; I also wanted to *become* Barbie and find my Ken and have my happy, rich cis straight white sex and life. For a long and painful time, I focused on that ideal – being Barbie and finding Ken – while rejecting who I was – who I am.

Over recent years, I have grown out of a-chieving that ideal through lessons learned from queer, disabled, Black, Indigenous, and other Communities of Color including my fellow vegans. Each day, I gain truths about myself, about what it means to be young, disabled, mestiza, and queer. Along my journey, I feel fortunate enough to have connected and learned from queer, vegans of color, especially Black queer vegan Christopher Sebastian McJetters. Last year, at a community-building event, focused on solidarity between veganism and other social justice movements, I had the joy of listening in person to some of my favorite queer vegans talk in a panel. It included Raffi Marhaba, Karla Rosa Vargas, and Jamila Alfred. One of the speakers gave the audience an important queer vegan lesson on compulsory heterosexuality and monogamy that I wished I knew then when I was four, eight, and definitely when I was 14. A panelist described a capitalistic notion exists in society that there is not enough love for everyone – that we are taught love is scarce, a resource not enough to produce and to go around. I believe they spoke this in response to single-issue activism both from vegans and non-vegans alike, who do not practice consistent anti-oppression that includes queer, disability, racial, economic, *and* animal liberation.

I further understood that when we embrace love as a scarce resource, we start to reject solidarity and community as oppressed beings and become careful to give and receive love. It becomes a commodity, a burden, and stripped of its healing and liberatory energy. If activism then becomes an expression of scarce love, then our activism becomes incomplete and siloed. As a disabled, queer Woman of Color, I experience very well how isolation becomes natural in spaces, and on the topic of love and activism, I find it natural to identify with words from Mia Mingus, a fellow disabled, queer Woman of Color, who writes,

> *Ableism and other systems of oppression and violence have left their mark on us. We can't on the one hand, understand how devastating capitalism, misogyny and criminalization are and then on the other hand, pretend as if they don't affect how we*

*treat each other and ourselves...isolation, exclusion, and erasure has been destructively wielded against us and our communities, so why would we want to wield them against each other? and if we can't love each other and ourselves, then what good is any of our work to get free?...One of the greatest way to resist abled supremacy [and other systemic oppressions] is by loving each other. How we were able to practice transformative love together in the face of fear, isolation, and heartbreak...This is how we practice interdependence...trust and belonging and hope. This is how we practice disability justice in its most powerful and magnificent potential.[2]*

So I write to you, non-Vegans of Color and non-vegan queers and even queer, Vegans of Color to also reject veganism as a commodity and embrace it as an act of love for non-human animals. I also write to you to reject single-issue activism and build community and solidarity with all movements towards liberation and justice. I write to myself to remember that accepting love – giving and receiving

---

[2]https://leavingevidence.wordpress.com/2018/11/03/
disability-justice-is-simply-another-term-for-love

– is a never-ending journey, one not limited to my activism but also in subverting my internalized queer antagonism and the ways that I have rejected and undervalued my attraction and love towards women.

As some queer vegans, especially Black, Ingenious, and other Vegans of Color may know, we are marginalized and oppressed from the antagonism of white mainstream veganism. But we are also alienated and isolated from our non-vegan social justice community who have also felt the antagonism, the isolation, fear, and heartbreak of white mainstream veganism and who are resistant to listening about veganism (and often, rightfully so) in the context of fat-shaming, greenwashing, diet culture, environmental injustice, and other systemic inequities. Their message also stayed with me many months later because as many activists, advocates, and organizers may know, social justice work is exhausting and can feel like constant never-ending battles; yet, we may forget the simple but radical act of expressing love and care for ourselves and our community. Although we are working within spaces of limited time, money, and other resources, love is a resource I never want to feel – or practice – in scarcity. That my love – and your love – is so abundant it can reach across prison abolition, reproductive/birth justice, anti-gentrification movements, disability justice, *and* include liberation for non-human animals and other social justice issues.

At four years old, I was powerless against the social practices of compulsory monogamy and heterosexuality. I wasn't fed with the image that maybe I could also be *with* Barbie...*and* Ken...*at the same time*. Or perhaps even more importantly, that I could be attracted to others who didn't embody the Kens and Barbies of the world because ultimately, they are products of white supremacy, disablist, and capitalist cis-hetero patriarchy. At four years old, I just knew Barbie for her beauty...her house...her convertible...and her equally good-looking man, Ken. I didn't know that it was okay to feel multiple types of attraction towards my girlfriends, or even multiple genders or multiple people, at the same time, and for all the years when I felt like the opposite of Barbie that it was okay to be the way I was. That I didn't have to hide B., J., A., M., P., and all the other girls and women in my life that I liked, flirted with, and touched. That my features, my culture, my skin, my class, my sensitivity, and my compassion towards the experiences of human animals and non-human animals, and my attraction to girls and boys were not weaknesses but all the source of my strength. That love and attraction come in many forms and that it is abundant for my community, friends,

87

family, partners, and advocacy.

Today, I am still striving to be unapologetic about my veganism and my belief that non-human animals also need liberation. I am learning to be resilient against the skepticism from fellow community members who have yet to confront their speciesism. I am also still venturing both in fear and love in exploring my truths and my maybe-truths under the bisexuality+ umbrella as a young, disabled Vegan of Color. And I don't know if maybe I will name, change, combine, or reject bi-, poly- or pansexual as my sexual identities – or maybe decide that queer and fem is enough; I invite myself to all possibilities.

I hope whoever is reading this rejects the belief that love is a scarce resource. Yes, our time and money are limited, and we are all called – or for some, left with no choice – to do social justice work for multiple reasons. And I know that many of you may center prison abolition, reproductive justice, disability, and queer justice in your activism. However, I urge you to continue to learn from queer, Vegans of Color. My world and my heart have expanded since I became a vegan almost five years ago. I wish you find that love, too, is abundant in your life to find solidarity with non-human animals in your activism.

## *The American Pipe Dream*

## Grayson Black

I am completely confounded as to what to do with my life. I am 23 years old and my passions have only broadened, my ardency only further oxygenized. For these 23 years I have experienced parallel lines of the same track, and in the past few years, I have taken a sledgehammer to both. Blow by blow, I have begun deconstructing that homosexuality is not wrong, and book by book, I have begun to eviscerate all the propagandic knowledge I have accrued during my life.

No, conversion counseling was certainly not the answer.

No, being gay is not morally unsound.

No, my lack of solid gender identity isn't a burden.

No, the Native Americans did not just relinquish their land and share their commodities  with European colonialists.

No, police are not the virtuous lighthouses my

white skin helped me to believe.

No, the United States did not save the world from Nazis during WWII.

But one of the biggest lies that I came out of the womb knowing was wrong, but was conditioned to sequester, was that non-human animals are for our own personal gain. Similarly, to my middle school sex-ed teachings and the insults spewed when walking down the street wearing makeup, I have had to eviscerate the norms and sanctions and create my own reality in a world rife with vitriol, exploitation, and objectification. These recent discoveries and revelations have flipped my world upside down more times than I can count, and now, now I am left reeling in my senior year of university. What can I do to make a difference without contributing to capitalism, globalization, climate change, and other endemic issues plaguing our very existence? After all, none of these issues are siloed, and animal rights are by proxy human rights. Is working for an NGO even effective when it promotes an annual $400 billion philanthropic capitalistic scheme within the United States? What job can I obtain where I have the platform to galvanize the fight against exploitation of migrant workers, the dispossession of indigenous peoples, rampant environmental degradation, water and food shortages in the Global South, the murder of endangered species encroaching on land of slaughterhouses, the superfluous slaughter of trillions of living beings, and the clandestine damnation of marginalized POCs through food deserts and covert redlining, and the simultaneous objectification of women through their consumerism? Moreover, how does one dismantle the system that allows all of these egregious acts to be possible?

It doesn't seem to be plausible. Society habitually prioritizes those that critically analyze one subject and work for niche industries but does not value those that possess polymathematical or interscholastic perspectives. Within capitalism, in order to keep a large machine running, there are many cogs for specific functions. This lack of visibility outside of one's own learnings allows capitalism to thrive as few rarely gain perspectives but of their own while also creating neo-aristocratic cadencies (doctors marry doctors, politicians marry politicians). The 1854 motifs of class struggles and disproportionate inequality in the novel Hard Times haven't vanished, but instead they have transformed. Unless truly searching, few are able to see this Dickensian nightmare that proliferates under the politics of sight.

While history has proven that the marginalized unsurprisingly seem to gather at the nexus of stigma-based solidarity, I still feel as though in order to be an effective advocate for queer folks, I must solely focus on queer issues. Additionally, veganism (along with being anti-establishment) in frequently deemed inflammatory and is alienating from those predominately white members of the LGBTQ+ community who paradoxically wield the most socioeconomic power. For even more within the gay community, animal-rights appears as moral pos-turing, yet one can actively witness these same gay cis-men chowing down on Chick-Fil-A and consuming products that conflate women with dead carcasses, and it leads to another worry...

Socrates identified knowledge with virtue. In order to be virtuous, one must carefully examine themselves and the world around them, while arguing dissimilar views. If this Socratic or dialectal methodology fails to incite people, and those with the knowledge remain the antitheses of virtue, then can apathy be combatted? If these members of the LGBTQ+ community know what they are contributing to and do nothing about it, then the chance of overturning the toxicity of the current world order seems especially arduous.

Nonetheless, with impending environmental

doom, the rise of fascism, and the augmentation of discord and xenophobia around the world comes a silver-lining: engagement. A time of pain has morphed into a time to heal old wounds and hinder upcoming problems. Feelings of anxiety have sparked thousands of protests across the nation, sparking other mass demonstrations across the seven seas. Hate and violence have brought dissimilar people together, while more and more artwork and literature are being cranked out. These pieces are not only purgative devices of uncertain times but also metaphorical weapons to electrify those downtrodden and those fighting for a better, kinder planet. And furthermore, environmental, economic, political, social, and bodily insecurity has catalyzed millions of people to consider not what the system is but how it can be. The dreams that I once had as a naïve child while I was being fed lies, self-hate, and animal carcasses have shifted. Like a vast ocean, they are reflecting the deeply penetrating glare of revolution.

FELIZ BRUECK AND McNEILL

## *Trans-cending the 'Man' and the Meat-Eater*

Doel Rakshit

CW: molestation, sexual harassment

A closet and a cage are manifestations of the same evil, the evil called oppression. I could not put this into words back when I was in the closet.

The mere sight of a static image of a cow being artificially inseminated by a farmer reverberated in my mind for a long time. It was a picture uploaded by a childhood friend of mine, Neerajan – a vocal and unapologetic keyboard activist. I knew he had turned vegan by then. I was aware of the term and the movement and was in the process of educating myself on the same. I would often criticize the vegan arguments in my mind and, at times, defend them too, creating an internal dialectic of conflicting thoughts. Yet, those sessions of internal debate did not bring about in me what this picture did – a paradigm shift. I looked at the cause with a whole new approach – a new lens that made much more sense to a closeted trans woman and demolished the ethnic lens of a human belonging to the Bengali community of India, known for its heavily meat-and-fish-eating habits across all castes.

The image made me feel empathy for the cow who was pictured being tortured by a stranger without their consent. It was a moment of utter shock. Until that moment, I wasn't aware that such a process existed in India; yet the farmer in the picture was visibly Indian. It triggered me, to say the least. As a consequence, all the experiences where I was molested and sexually harassed by uninvited people started playing in my mind like a slideshow. This was the beginning of my vegan journey.

When I look back at those days of me trying hard to bring about a radical change in my consumption patterns and being vocal about nonhuman animals on social media (this is usually where the activist's debut happens nowadays), I can see a trans woman – herself suffering in a closet – addressing the sufferings of those in cages, too, because of a consumption system collectively supported by her species. She didn't have the courage to come out of her closet back then. It was difficult. The invisibility of trans women except in trains and traffic signals "begging" for a living always discouraged her to come out and dream of a mainstream life. These women she saw were from traditional transgender communities known as Hijra, Aravani, Kinnar, etc. They joined these co-mmunities to stay protected; begging was their only source of income. The oppressive history of her community was never far from her mind, yet somehow, she felt liberated while protesting against oppression of nonhuman animals and demanding their total liberation. Without her conscious knowledge, her trans identity became the driving force behind her participation in nonhuman animal rights activism.

On my first day of street activism, when the National Animal Rights Day (NARD) was being observed in Mumbai, I didn't have any idea that someday I would possibly gather courage to come out as who I am. It was through recurrent active participation in voicing the sufferings of the oppressed other that I, unknowingly, became fearless enough to voice the sufferings of my oppressed self. My activism made me ready to subvert in a stronger way, building my self-confidence to eventually come out of my closet which was a form subversion in the face of the cis-hetero-patriarchal system. After almost two years of being a vegan and activist I decided it was time for me to live my life as my authentic self – a woman.

So, was it my trans identity that made me go vegan and join activism? Or was it my veganism that made me confident enough to break out of my closet? A big yes — for both. While my own sufferings made me empathize with the sufferings of and oppression against nonhuman animals, the open and unapologetic stance that I took against the same made me capable of going beyond the boundaries of my closet that the society had burdened me with.

In essence, the trans woman in me made me go vegan, and the vegan in me helped me come out.

## *Dual Identities: Feminist, Vegan, and LGBTQIA+*

Kanika Sud

One might assume that being vegan *and* being an LGBTQIA+ person do not have much in common. However, the more I think about it, the more these two aspects of my life seem to be intertwined.

I identify as a pro-intersectional feminist, vegan, and an LGBTQIA+ person – a bisexual cis woman, to be precise. Personally, I'm quite fond of other animals (or nonhuman persons, as I like to call them). I'm the kind of person who sees a cute pupper or kitty and gets an uncontrollable urge to cuddle them. If one is friends with me on Facebook, one will notice how my timeline is inundated with cute and funny puppy, goat, or pig videos. I'm appreciative of the existence of non-human species, and I recognize their individuality although I do understand that one does not need to love or appreciate non-human species to respect their existence.

That being said, I believe in equality, and I cannot confidently say that we have accomplished equality for ALL – be it humans or nonhumans. It is a controversial statement to make, which may receive a lot of backlash given the complex socio-political realities in India. India is a casteist[3] society and many still consider it laughable when topic of nonhuman animal rights is brought up for discussion as it is considered either trivial or elitist and casteist. However, Prateek Kumar (2019), in his essay entitled *The Intersection of Casteism and Spe-ciesism: Interconnections from a Dalit*[4], challenges this notion. Kumar articulates that Indian society is deeply rooted in casteism, despite the changes brought about in legislation, and establishes the notion that nonhuman animal oppression is one of the major ways in which casteism was allowed to take root and continue to this day. In essence, casteist speciesism allows for the exploitation of castes through a hierarchy that makes it clear that the notion of justice and equality must extend to all humans AND nonhuman species if we are to address other forms of marginalization that hold India back.

I was born in the Bania caste[5] to a Hindu family originally from Himachal Pradesh, India. Professio-

---

[3]A system of oppression where the caste system is adhered.
[4]Please refer to *Veganism of Color*: Decentering Whiteness in Human and Nonhuman Liberation, edited by Julia Feliz Brueck in 2019
[5]One of the Privileged/ Upper Castes in India. It is an Occupational community of merchants, bankers, dealers in

nally, they were involved in money lending, dealing with grains, spices, and so forth. Food habits in the Hinterlands of Himachal Pradesh are different from Mainland India. Given the cold climatic conditions in Himachal Pradesh, most people in the region resort to consuming animal meat and secretions (like my paternal grandparent's home, I've been told). Many Banias in the mainland of India, however, practice vegetarianism[6]. Both my parents and their families shifted to Chandigarh and Delhi, and later we shifted to Muscat, Oman. I was raised in a vegetarian household by my parents in Muscat, Oman. My parents, however, never strictly imposed vegetarianism on their children. Despite that, I chose to not participate in consuming animal meat, as I always believed in expressing compassion towards nonhuman species. Hence, I have been a vegetarian for most of my life, which I believed, aligned with my personal affinity towards non-human species despite vegetarianism being something done by privileged castes to maintain caste purity.

---

grains and spices and in modern times, numerous commercial enterprises.

[6]Prateek Kumar's essay elaborately highlights how vegetarianism is practiced by the privileged castes to maintain caste purity.

Through my vegetarianism, I believed I wasn't contributing to the atrocities forced on other nonhuman species because I was rejecting animal flesh in my diet and clothing. However, having learned about the ways female farmed animals are brutalized for their milk, I stopped consuming dairy and dairy products in 2016. Like any other woman or person with a uterus, I can empathize with what it feels like to be dominated, violated by force, and in a way, consumed. Although people from across gender and sexual orientation spectra experience sexual violations, myriads of statistics demonstrate that LGBTQIA+ persons are more likely to experience physical violence based on their sexual identity.

Having understood all this, seeing women and other LGBTQIA+ folks consume animal products induces sadness in me. As women and people with uteri, especially queer womxn, we are quite familiar with the asymmetrical power relations which perpetuate violence in a system that benefits from abusing and slaughtering nonhuman species, especially those that are female-assigned.

The notion that abusing cows, chickens, goats, sheep for food and clothing is acceptable while abusing cats and dogs is not is based on a fractured worldview that nonhumans used for food are less worthy of compassion and justice. I sense that biphobia, transphobia, sexism, casteism, ableism (and any other system of oppression) work on the same logic. Just like how we "otherize" certain segments of marginalized populations to dominate and exploit them, we do the same to nonhuman species. We bully them, kill them, and use them for our benefit because our society and culture conditions us to consider them as unworthy of our care and ideas of justice. Nonhuman species are so victimized that we don't even notice they are victims! This is one of the reasons why I as a cis-woman and part of the LGBTQIA+ community feel that we must organize and mobilize ourselves to actively speak against speciesism[7], for our fellow nonhuman species, in the same way that we speak up against our own oppressions. It is pertinent to stand in solidarity with all victims of abuse and exploitation and to advocate for justice with and for them.

I understand, not everyone has the luxury of multiple options, given that many segments of the population live in dire poverty, and many queer folks leave home to escape from abuse they face.

---

[7]The term speciesism was coined in 1970 by animal rights proponent Richard D. Ryder to argue that granting humans more rights than animals is an irrational prejudice. The term was popularized in 1975 by the philosopher Peter Singer.

Still, animal rights are an issue that affects us all. Leather, meat, dairy industries, and so on exploit the people from the marginalized castes and classes creating a health crisis for them through the horrendous effects of working in these toxic spaces.

Recently, I came across a fellow cis, bi-romantic non-vegan woman, who was vacillating with the idea of adopting veganism. From her personal research, she was distraught to know about the atrocities that are impinged upon non-humans for leather, milk, eggs, meat, and so on. Having rescued a dog earlier, she began understanding nonhumans and their expressions better. This enabled her to relate to other nonhuman species too, which she earlier only thought as food. However, she wondered if the humane consumption of nonhuman products was possible. She also cited unavailability of plant-based products in her hometown, or, if they were available, they were inaccessible due to their inflated prices. I clarified to her that simple vegetarian meal without "ghee" and "dahi" (milk products used extensively in India) are easily accessible and enough to fulfill one's nutritional requirement (something she was quite anxious about). I've been in touch in her and numerous others to assist them in their journey towards veganism as I feel it is my responsibility to guide others where I can when we have the choice to reduce the injustices forced on others regardless of the accessibility that is currently available for others.

This brings me to those that are already vegan or plant-based: if we really want veganism to be all inclusive (which it currently is not), the questions we must raise in India are: how do we bring a shift within systems and structures that normalize consumption of non-human bodies and their secretions? What can we do to make plant-based food and products more accessible to everyone? At a theory and a praxis level, how could veganism and the nonhuman animal rights movement prioritize *consistent anti-oppression*[8] activism? Importantly, how can feminist/queer/anti-caste theory and politics inform vegan activism?

Kumar (2018), a Dalit vegan, explains that *"casteist speciesism"* allows overt and covert caste-based discrimination to continue unhindered. Through this relationship, speciesism renders some nonhumans more valuable and sacred as opposed to others along the caste lines. For instance, cows

---

[8]Term borrowed from Julia Feliz, author and editor of *Veganism in an Oppressive World.* The author speaks of promoting veganism as a whole and not in pieces. It should not be a movement just to "save" nonhumans while adding to the oppression of the marginalized people.

are known as "Gau Mata" (Holy mother); pigs are associated with dirt and filth and nowhere associated with the "upper caste" people; horses are the pride and property of the warrior castes in India; and so on. Therefore, lower caste people are not permitted to ride horses and camels. Adding to this, dairy and dairy products are considered holy, hence consumed by upper caste vegetarians, while animal meat is considered the food of the devil and thus associated with lower castes. In her essay *Animal Liberation is a Feminist Issue*, Poojari (2017) further articulates how a larger culture plays on the idea that power has to be exercised over the physically weak. She explains how an all-pervasive patriarchal culture enables the normalization of oppression and exploitation, especially if you are born or identify as a female. Casteism, patriarchy, and speciesism are all intersecting systems of oppressions where we deny those at the other end of an asymmetrical power spectrum of their subjectivity. They are victimized to such an extent that they are not rendered victims. As Aph Ko (2017), co-author of *Aphro-ism: Essays on Pop Culture, Feminism, and Black Veganism from Two Sisters* highlights, "The objectification of animals has been so successful that they are entirely stripped of their subjectivity: They exist for us." Thus, it is in our and animals' best interest to challenge these systemic oppressions which normalizes oppressions on both human and

nonhuman bodies and deems consumption of
nonhuman bodies and secretions acceptable.

One of the many ways of challenging speciesism is making plant-based food and products
accessible to everyone. We must advocate for a
more accessible and just food system where every
healthy plant-based product is made the norm and
food is grown in such a way that all inhabitants of all
countries benefit from it. One may assume that only
our doctors and nutritionists guide us on what to
eat and what to not. However, food trends are far
more political and economically as well as culturally
motivated than one may assume. Cohen and Leroy
(2019)[9] in their essay articulate that food has been
at the center of economy and this can be seen from
the time of Ancient Rome when provision of bread
to citizens was seen as a measure of good
government[10] to Adam Smith[11] highlighting a link
between wages and the price of corn. They further

---

[9]https://scroll.in/article/946528/the-real-winner-in-the-
growth-of-veganism-is-capitalism
[10]Please refer to *Frumentariae Leges* by W. Smith for an
elaborate understanding of how supply of corn to the people
was seen as a duty of the government.
[11]Adam Smith was an Economist who wrote an influential book
*The Wealth of Nations* (1776). He was a vital proponent of
Laissez- Faire Economic Policies. Smith created the concept of
what is now known as Gross Domestic Product (GDP).

write that Marx[12] had declared too, that food is at the center of all political structures. He advised against an alliance of industry and capital intent on controlling food production which would work against the poor and the marginalized. Saryta Rodriguez (2018), an editor of *Food Justice: A Primer*[13], examined food justice from different aspects – economical, environmental, ethical, and social. Her book also highlights how non-human agriculture is an injustice to nonhumans and humans alike, while also destroying the planet. The humans working in non-human industries (be it for food, leather, and so on) are subject to terrible conditions and low wages globally.

We find the same is true in India. Kumar (2017) reiterates and elaborates how casteist speciesism in India rendered Dalits and lower castes in India to work in these toxic animal-based industries which are detrimental to their health. They are given the job of slaughtering animals, removing the dead skin off them, cleaning, and drying it for leather. All leather industries are filled with Dalit workers or "lower class" Muslims who are destined to work on

---

[12]Marx was a Political economist and socialist revolutionary who moved away from philosophy and towards political economics. His work thoroughly inspired the foundation of many communist regimes.
[13]Food Justice: A Primer by Saryta Rodriguez

contractual basis simply due to their caste. Therefore, it is imperative to re-emphasize Kumar's concluding points, which establish the reality of how human and non-human oppression in India is linked, and therefore adopting veganism would contribute in destabilizing the deeply rooted casteist speciesism in India.

Revisiting the questions, "how could veganism and the animal rights movement prioritize *consistent anti-oppression* activism?" and how can Feminist/Queer/Anti-Caste theory and politics inform vegan activism? I'd like to share the methodologies of Sanctuary Publishers[14], which emphasize that without working on root issues that make veganism accessible beyond the privileged, we won't be able to achieve nonhuman liberation. This is the same for other movements including the LGBTQIA+ one. We cannot move forward without understanding root issues, which form the basis of the oppressive systems we are also affected by, and how they relate to the oppression of all others.

---

[14]Please refer to: www.consistentantioppression.com/ the-why-what/methodologies for detailed reading of methodologies with examples for further clarification.

## *On Being (Un)Natural: Queer Veganism and the Appeal to Nature*

S. Marek Muller, PhD


Veganism is, at its core, a critique and reformation of what it means to be a member of a broader moral community. Since speciesism centers the *homo sapiens* in this community, I understand questions of nonhuman animal ethics and queer identity as interrogations of what it means to be a *human* versus what it means to be an *animal*. And, since the rhetorical construction of the human relies on its opposition to the nonhuman, the animal, the wild, or the natural, to understand speciesism is to simultaneously understand what it means to exist in relation to capital-N *Nature.*

At the same time, I cannot separate my veganism from my queerness. To be queer—to deviate from the heterosexist (heterosexuality > other sexualities) and cissexist (cisgender > transgender) standards of a dominant culture—is not only an embodied argument against cultural norms but also a critique of biological determinism (DeCecco & Elia 1993). That is to say, my existence as a queer human calls into question normative understandings of what the human body is, does, or should do in order to adequately perform its Humanness.

As a communication researcher, I specialize in identifying argumentative minutiae that are seemingly meaningless but are upon closer inspection fundamental to creation and the maintaining oppressive norms. Today, as I reflect upon my asexuality and my gender ambiguity, I remember the battle to *identify* myself the subsequent pain of *accepting* myself. "Neither of these are real things," I said. "If they were, some doctor would have told you about them by now." It took years and years to accept that my sexual and gender identities were, in fact, valid. It took much longer to figure out why I couldn't accept them. Upon reflection, however, I realized why I always thought I "couldn't" be who I was, why my gender nonconformity and my aceness were not "real." Simply, the reason came down to the argumentative tropes that I study on a day-to-day basis. More specifically, I could not understand or accept myself as queer due to an argumentative fallacy foundational to structural oppression: the Appeal to Nature.

What do I mean by an Appeal to Nature? Before defining that argumentative fallacy, let's go back a couple of steps. As animal rights advocates

and activists committed to consistent anti-
oppression, it is quite easy to identify how comparing humans to nonhuman animals is used to
oppress the former through an analogy to the latter.
We see it all the time. Just look at the Trump
administration's consistent comparisons of migrants
to insects and their subsequent detention and
maltreatment. According to speciesist standards,
Humans > Nonhuman Animals. Through the use of
dualistic rhetoric, the Human/Animal binary affords
aspects of "Culture" to humans that, through
advances in cognition, reasoning, creativity, and
technology, separate them from uncivilized and
brutish Nature. Ergo, if Humans > Nonhumans, then
it is also true that Culture > Nature. To be compared
to an animal is thus to be expelled from civilized
society and into the wild, to have one's membership
in the moral community be cast aside (Haslam, et al.
2007). To be human is to be cultured and to be
cultured is to be happily Unnatural. To be Unnatural
is to have progressed beyond the limitations of
mere animality and developed complex societies,
relationships, and technologies (Kimaid 2019). Thus,
Unnatural > Natural. To understand the rhetoric of
speciesism is to understand the following
argumentative schema: Humans > Nonhuman Animals *because* Culture > Nature *because* Unnatural >
Natural.

This schema and its applications are simple enough to see in everyday life. Look, for instance, at the hot-button arguments over GMO's versus organic foods, which are, at their core, competing questions of if humans can, or even should, make natural organisms better than nature "naturally" makes itself (Downing 2011). Or look at international development efforts to bring Western industrialized agriculture to rural African communities in an effort to make their food production and consumption practices more mechanized in order to transition their food cultures from "developing" subsistence to "developed" excess (Banerjee 2003). Better yet, look at the history of the violent colonization and exploitation of non-Western societies, particularly how such practices were predicated upon and justified by presumptions of European-ness being the ultimate form of Humanness (Wynter 2003).

So where does the Appeal to Nature fit into this rhetorical mess? We're getting closer now. As I followed this argumentative schema, I noticed an inconsistency. Regarding Nature and its inherent non-Humanness, this weird thing happened when gender identities and sexual orientations came into the mix. Suddenly, these identities and orientations were invalid (they were perversions or they did not exist at all) because, well, I suppose if we had to come up with a reason...Nature? That is to say, the prevailing rationale for my non-existence was that if some version of myself did not exist in Nature, then it did not exist at all in me. But wait one moment. If humans are, by the aforementioned argumentative schema, *not* Nature, when how on earth was I supposed to interpret and respond to this cognitive dissonance, to this rhetorical reversal?

To answer the above question, let's finally define the Appeal to Nature. According to argumentation experts, there are multiple "rules" for and "patterns" applies in persuasive arguments. Many of these patterns come in the form of "appeals," such as *pathos* (an appeal to emotion), *logos* (an appeal to logic), and *ethos* (an appeal to the credibility of the arguer themselves). An appeal is a natural product of argumentation since they form the "reasons" that support a thesis. For example, perhaps one reason my word can be trusted in my examination of queer veganism is because of my triple identity as a rhetorician, a queer person, and a vegan. This would be an appeal to my own *ethos.* These terms and theories come straight out of the early works of Greek philosophers like Aristotle and Plato and have lasted through the ages.

Appeals are natural and normal facets of arguments. They are not inherently good or bad. However, when appeals are used in a manner that block substantive arguments from occurring, they become what is known as a "fallacy" (van Eemeren & Grootendorst 2016). Fallacies are, basically, bad arguments. They are bad because they are nonsensical. Some of them most of us have heard of in some form or another, for instance, the *ad hominem* where I attack the character of the arguer instead of responding to their actual arguments (you tell me that I shouldn't do something because it is homophobic and I retort that your opinion is invalid since you are a known asshole).

As I examined my internalized hatred of myself and my queerness, I scrutinized a very particular and very problematic type of appeal: the Appeal to Nature. This appeal has another name that is much more indicative of its problems: the "Naturalistic Fallacy" (Daston 2014, Trebilcot 1975). The argumentative structure of a Naturalistic Fallacy goes as follows: *x* exists in Nature, and therefore, it is acceptable. On the surface, this type of argument seems valid. If something exists outside of the scope of human culture, then it makes perfect sense that this would be a good claim to defend claims about gender and sexuality. Indeed, one of the premier defenses of queer culture prior to the legalization of gay marriage was that we queers were, to use Lady Gaga's preferred terminology, "born this way." Queerness was Nature, not Nurture. Ergo, it was acceptable.

Why, then, is the Appeal to Nature so dangerous, so fallacious? Well, let's take a look at how it has been used in the opposite direction by anti-queer voices. Homophobes, biphobes, aphobes, and transphobes have worked for eons to deny queer identities by framing differential gender and sexual performances as a "choice" (Nurture, not Nature). Animals weren't queer, so neither were humans. Animals didn't have nonbinary genders, so neither did humans. Animals naturally and instinctively reproduce and have babies, therefore humans should, too. Want to argue against it? Then I guess the onus is now on the biologists to prove that there are gay penguins. How frustrating for me. As a gender ambiguous asexual, what precisely was I supposed to be emulating? A "real" asexual being? A cell? An amoeba?

This reasoning perturbed me as I got older and continued to interrogate my seemingly unnatural and thus bad and thus unwanted existence. At the time, I truly did not care if nonhuman animals also had diverse sexualities. Although biologists, ecologists, and cognitive ethologists have long since proved that other species are *not*, in fact, solely heterosexual beings (Poiani 2010), presumptions of nonhuman heteronorma- tivity were not what was perturbing me. What bothered me was the hypocrisy. The contradiction. The cognitive dissonance. What grinded my gears was that the only reason heterosexuality was THE sexuality was because it was, well, *natural*. In this new argument schema, Humans = Nature. Heterosexuality = Natural. Ergo, Heterosexuality = Human. Therefore, Natural > Unnatural. To be queer, therefore, was to be unnatural, and to be unnatural was to be nonhuman, and to be nonhuman was to be, well, *bad*. It made no sense. The entire premise of speciesism, after all, relied upon the total opposite argumentative framework.

So here we are at last. The reason that the Appeal to Nature is fallacious is because it is *utterly incoherent*. One minute, Humans are supposed to be better than, or totally separate from, Nature. According to the logic of white supremacy, one had best assimilate into the cultural norms of capital-W Whiteness lest one be associated with subhuman savagery. The next minute, however, Humans had best abide by Nature lest they become perverted social deviants. According to the principles of heteronormativity, for instance, I had best take medications to boost my libido in order to fix my missing natural desire to partner up and procreate.

Why on earth does this fallacious appeal function so efficiently? I was flabbergasted and confused as I worked through the knotted arguments. But I guess it starts to make sense when we begin to assess "Nature" as an arbitrary social construct. Nature is not "real." Its separation from humanity is not "real." Rather, these separations and overlaps are discursively modeled and remodeled over and over to meet the needs of the rhetor (Cronon 1996).

And here we see the connection to animal liberation, to veganism, to consistent anti-oppression. Animals are presumed to be part of this socially constructed definition of Nature. They're just as implicated as we are. Running through my culture are completely arbitrary utilizations of what is Natural (for instance: eating meat, being heterosexual, hunting animals, having babies) and therefore what is *right*. At the same exact moment, I am told through the logic of speciesism that to engage with my Naturalness is undesirable (for instance: being "emotional" as opposed to "rational" or being described with whatever "animalistic" character trait could be used at any moment me my agency). I am bombarded with characterizations of what is Unnatural and therefore Human and therefore Desirable (for instance: my iPhone, my car, my English language skills—whatever "separates man from the beasts" today). Concurrently, I am warned of what is Unnatural and Human and therefore Undesirable (for instance: whatever aspect of human identity upsets societal norms this morning, like my asexuality, my not wanting to have sex with you, your sister, or anyone else).

I believe that I would still be queer even if I was not vegan. I believe I would still be vegan even if I was not queer. But I believe that I am much better at both of those things because of the intersections of queerness and veganism. To be queer is to consistently battle against our dehumanization within a heterosexist and cissexist environment. To be vegan is to battle against the animalization and subsequent exploitation of nonhuman sentient subjects. Queer veganism is to notice the intersections of these oppressions; it is to notice the inherent contradictions of binaries like Human/Nonhuman Animal, Culture/Nature, and Natural/Unnatural; and finally, it is to put the principles of queer and animal liberation into practice through education, advocacy, and activism committed to consistent anti-oppression.

*Cited Works*

Banerjee, S. B. (2003). Who sustains whose development? Sustainable development and the reinvention of nature. *Organization studies*, 24(1), 143-180.

Cronon, W. (1996). The trouble with wilderness. *Environmental history*, 1(1), 20-25.

Daston, L. (2014). The naturalistic fallacy is modern. *Isis*, 105(3), 579-587.

DeCecco, J. P., & Elia, J. P. (1993). A critique and synthesis of biological essentialism and social constructionist views of sexuality and gender. *Journal of Homosexuality*, 24(3-4), 1-26.

Downing, D. (2011). Narrative exchange as knowledge transfer: The rhetorical construction of opposition to GM Crops in SW England. *Anthropology Matters*, 13(1), 1-12.

Frankena, W. K. (1939). The naturalistic fallacy. *Mind*, 48(192), 464-477.

Haslam, N., Loughnan, S., Reynolds, C., & Wilson, S. (2007). Dehumanization: A new perspective. *Social and Personality Psychology Compass*, 1(1), 409-422.

Kimaid, M. (2019). The language of power: Science, statecraft, and words. *Historical Encounters*, 6(1), 40-53.

Poiani, A. (2010). *Animal homosexuality: a biosocial perspective*. Cambridge University Press.

Trebilcot, J. (1975). Sex roles: The argument from nature. *Ethics*, 85(3), 249-255.

Van Eemeren, F. H., & Grootendorst, R. (2016). *Argumentation, communication, and fallacies: A pragma-dialectical perspective*. Routledge.

Wynter, S. (2003). Unsettling the coloniality of being/power/truth/freedom: Towards the human, after man, its overrepresentation—An argument. *CR: The new centennial review*, 3(3), 257-337.

## *Let's Go Outside: Thoughts on Queer Veganism*

Margaret Robinson, PhD

I remember the moment I began identifying as two-spirit. It was Spring, and I was walking along Queen's Park in Toronto, looking at the tiny blue flowers that are the first to bloom there. I'd developed a solid identity as a bisexual and queer woman and found community and activism and friends, but I realized that my identity as a Mi'kmaw woman hadn't undergone the same growth. I decided to join a group for two-spirit people at the Native Canadian Centre on Spadina Road run by two-spirit elder Blu Waters. I connected with community and found a Mi'kmaw elder working in Toronto. Since then my identity as a Mi'kmaw woman and my understanding of my two-spirit identity has grown and deepened.

My home is in the traditional and unceded territory of the Mi'kmaq on the Northeastern coast of what is currently Canada. I'm home again after 20 years in Toronto for school and work. In the Summer of 2008, I went vegan (see Robinson & Corman 2017). Since then, I've tried to relate my veganism to my Indigenous teachings and cultural values. Sometimes this is easy since my culture is clear that every animal is a some*one* instead of some*thing*. The Mi'kmaq tend to see other animals as our relatives, expressed in the phrase "Msit No'kmaq," which means "all my relations." At other times finding a connection between being vegan and being Mi'kmaq is difficult such as when I think about the diet of my ancestors, 90% of which came from other animals (McMillan 2018). Being vegan separates me from the practices of other Mi'kmaq, but I firmly believe it's in keeping with our cultural values.

In my work life, I'm an assistant professor at Dalhousie University, and although I do write on veganism and also on sexuality and gender, I'd never related these topics to one another. So I'm grateful to Julia Feliz for inviting me to reflect on that. I welcome the opportunity to consider how my queerness connects to veganism and how it can help me escape European settler binaries to live a less colonized life. In this essay, I examine the work of two scholars of second-wave feminism, a movement that began in 1960 and lasted until the late 1980s. It's the feminism my mother had, and it's the type I first encountered. At a psychology conference in Washington DC, listening to an older lesbian feminist, I realized we had very different experiences of second-wave feminism—it gave her community and put a voice to experiences of oppression she hadn't had language to describe. To me, it felt sex-negative, inflexible, dominating, and excluding—especially of me as a bisexual and of my trans allies. I was born in 1973, so I'm a member of Generation X and feel drawn to third wave feminism's exploration of how categories meet, merge, or overlap. But even as "waves" of feminism describe something real, they are also arbitrary and artificial. These waves don't capture my experience of Indigenous feminism, which Michi Saagiig Nishnaabeg scholar Leanne Simpson has called "no wave" feminism (see Simpson's quote in Ahmad 2015).

It's not difficult to see connections between colonialism and the use and spread of European-style animal agriculture. Large areas of arable soil are needed to support settler food animals such as cattle and sheep and to grow the crops that feed those animals. As settler numbers increase, Indigenous people are forced off (and in some cases starved off) our territories to make way for settler farm homesteads. Displacement of Indigenous nations and animals to make way for settler farming and ranching is the history of "The American West" but is also happening on a global scale (Weis 2013). To obtain the agreements that made some of these land grabs possible, Indigenous women were removed from positions of power in politics and in

Indigenous food economies by settler policies that forced patriarchal political structures onto Indigenous nations. So, for example, many women lost the right to hold political positions, to vote, and women were pushed out of their leadership roles in farming as Indigenous men were groomed to mimic European peasant farmers. Given this history, there are clear connections between the oppression of Indigenous women, the stealing of Indigenous territory, and the oppression of non-human animals within settler agricultural industries. Anticolonial theorist Andrea Smith has detailed how settlers use stolen land, stolen labour, and force against groups and nations perceived as different, in order to support heteronormativity—the elevation of heterosexuality as the only natural way of being sexual. In what is currently North America, settler practices were also Christian practices, and Indigenous nations were forced to change their political structures, family structures, gender systems, sexual practices, and sustainable food practices to conform to European morality. Residential schools in Canada and boarding schools in the United States nearly obliterated Indigenous cultures and the Indigenous languages in which opposition to colonial thought could be expressed or dissent fomented. I have detailed the role that cultural erasure schooling and forced Christianization had in erasing Indigenous gender systems elsewhere (Robinson 2019 a and b) but have not connected gender or sexuality with veganism more explicitly until now. In examining gender and sexuality in connection to veganism, there are ideas in second-wave lesbian feminist theory that I find promising, especially for how they deconstruct settler practices (though they don't call them that explicitly).

## Adrienne Rich: *Compulsory Heterosexuality and Lesbian Existence*

Adrienne Rich's ground-breaking essay (1980), examines how heterosexuality is treated as 'natural,' yet also as requiring constant social reinforcement with those who stray from straightness being punished in significant ways. Rich explains how across a range of male-dominated academic fields, partnering with men is framed as essential for women's fulfilment *as women*:

> *...the social sciences...asserts that primary love between the sexes is "normal," that women need men as social and economic protectors, for adult sexuality, and for psychological completion; that the heterosexually constituted family is the basic social unit; that women who do not attach their primary intensity to men*

*must be, in functional terms, condemned to an even more devastating out-siderhood than their outsiderhood as women* (Rich 1980, p. 657).

I encounter the assumptions Rich outlines above in nearly every sphere in which I live and work. Within psychology, for example, bisexual women are over-diagnosed with borderline personality disorder. The criteria for this disorder includes "a pattern of unstable and intense interpersonal relationships," and "markedly and persistently unstable self-image or sense of self" (American Psychiatric Association 2013). Kate Harrad, the author of *Purple Prose: Bisexuality in Britain*, notes that when psychiatrists assume that being straight is the healthiest and most stable way of relating, it causes women's bisexuality to be taken as evidence of borderline personality disorder. More broadly, I notice a tendency to naturalize heterosexuality by assuming that other sexualities need an explanation or cause while being straight does not. I am rarely asked, "When did your attraction to men manifest?" yet I'm often asked to detail the emergence of my attraction to women or non-binary people as if the truth of my identity can be found in an origin story. I find Rich's article to be useful for counters claims like these, that heterosexuality is "natural."

In a course called Living Queer as Indigenous Women, I use Rich's essay to introduce students to the idea that the categories most people think of as natural are created and maintained through specific types of power relations. Understanding how power shapes gender is a good primer for examining how colonial governments shape and deform Indigenous gender systems. The power system Rich examines is heteropatriarchy—a system of ruling that privileges straight men over all others. Rich argues that the imperative to partner with men "has been both forcibly and subliminally imposed on women" (1980, p. 653). By outlining the costs of refusing heterosexuality and detailing efforts to prevent women from imagining alternatives to partnering with men, Rich invites the reader to wonder, "if heterosexuality is innate, why is it be so heavily enforced?"

Like heterosexuality, meat-eating is also presented as inevitable and natural. Proponents of carnivorism often point to our earliest human relatives, whose habits are expected to reveal hidden truths about how humans should eat today. Some even imagine that meat-eating is what distinguished humans from other animals in our evolutionary history (Stanford 1999; Wrangham 2009). This excerpt from the work of Paul Jordan summarized that position well:

*Meat eating provided more energy more readily and economically than a vegetarian diet could ever do and it has been ingeniously proposed that it went hand in hand with brain enlargement; to preserve the metabolic balance overall, as the energy demanding brain expanded with evolution, the gut could be usefully reduced in size through the eating of energy-rich meat. On this proposal, meat eating was the sine qua non of brain development, upon which natural selection set such a premium for the sake of cleverness in social behaviour and resourcefulness in survival and reproduction* (Jordan 2001).

Regardless of any role meat is imagined to have in human development, it plays a central role in North America's food industries. The governments of United States and Canada support the meat and dairy industries through farm subsidy programs and promote their products in food guides produced by the United States Department of Agriculture since 1919 and the Canadian Council on Nutrition since 1942. Such guides frame animal products as constituting "food groups" such as "meat and fish," "dairy," and "eggs," which they describe as essential for nutrition (Government of Canada, 2019; United States Department of Agriculture, 2011). The promotion of meat and dairy is so standard that when Canada's 2019 Food Guide was released, most news stories about it expressed shock that dairy and meat appeared to play a smaller role than in previous years (Hughes, 2019, McCue 2019) with one headline asking, "Where's the beef? Industry stakeholders cry foul over Health Canada food guide freeze-out" (Jolsom, 2018).

Just as Rich questions heterosexuality, we might wonder how "natural" meat-eating is if it requires constant advertising. Lobby groups such as Dairy Farmers of Canada, Egg Farmers of Canada, and the Canadian Meat Council have long run ad campaigns associating their products with freshness, nutrition, and a rural middle-class lifestyle they frame as wholesome. This promotion is paired with the stigmatizing of people who do not consume animal products. One advertisement by Dairy Farmers of Canada read, "Real milk comes from real cows. Anything else is nuts." The campaign plays on the double-meaning of "nuts" to evoke the stigma attached to mental illness and project it onto people who choose nut-based milks (such as almond) over dairy.

Vegan challenges to claims that eating animals is natural can be seen in a number of places. People for the Ethical Treatment of Animals (PETA) countered naturalizing in a Twitter post: "You put a baby in a crib w/ an apple & a rabbit. If it eats the rabbit & plays w/ the apple, I'll buy you a new car" (PETA 2015). Even as "paleo" diets were all the rage, an article on the *Scientific American* blog argued, "Human Ancestors Were Nearly All Vegetarians" (Dunn 2012). Yet these efforts pale in comparison to the commercial forces working to naturalize the use of animal products. When my niece was born, I was shocked by how many toys for children normalize animal agriculture (looking at you, Little People® Caring for Animals Farm). These companies also portray Indigenous people as historical rather than contemporary. Playmobil, for example, sells "Native American" playsets whose figures carry bows, arrows, and spears. While challenging the framing of meat-eating as "natural" is important, conversations about nature often evoke the example of Indigenous people in ways that frame us as pre-historic rather than contemporary. This has strong negative impacts on Indigenous land claim cases, making us seem either extinct or inauthentic and therefore ineligible to claim our own territory.

Another aspect of Rich's essay I find useful are the insights into how sexuality and gender intersect when it comes to demands on our time and resources. Rich argues that women are expected to provide sexual, emotional, and economic labour to men as a function of being female. I see a similar dynamic in the emotional labour that Indigenous people are expected to do in first explaining colonialism to settlers, then proving that it's bad, and finally supporting settlers through their guilt pangs. As a vegan, I am sometimes expected to reassure omnivores that they're still "good people." Women who refuse emotional labour to men are framed as unfeminine; vegans who refuse emotional labour to omnivores are labelled as judgemental; and Indigenous people who refuse emotional labour to settlers are framed as "difficult."

Demands that the oppressed contribute to the wellbeing of their oppressors are coupled with demands about how our subordination is performed. Rich examines how gender and sexuality overlap, noting that workplaces require lesbians to perform subordinate femininity in order to pass not only as straight but also as women:

> *A lesbian, closeted on her job because of heterosexist prejudice, is not simply forced into denying the truth of her outside relationships or private life; her job depends on her pretending to be not merely heterosexual but a heterosexual woman, in terms of dressing and playing the feminine, deferential role required*

*of "real" women* (Rich 1980, p. 642).

As settler practices erased our self-expression as Indigenous people, we are increasingly expected to perform our Indigeneity in specific ways or risk not being read as Indigenous at all. We sometimes refer to these expected roles as "the four Ds": drumming, dancing, drinking, and dying. The masquerade Rich describes also raises questions for me about gender in relation to veganism. As someone whose training was in theology, I see connections between how women have been framed as less than human, and as subordinate to men (the superior and more rational being), just as other animals are subordinated to humans.

The field of mental health takes many of its ideas about health from religion. One 19th century idea called "degeneration theory" suggested that due to increasing industrialization humans were under new and greater stressors than before. Such stressors, degenerationalists believed, put pressure on society until individuals with "poor genetics" broke, becoming bestial, antisocial, and criminal. Some thought a return to "clean living" would counteract this problem. Adherents of degeneration theory, such as Richard von Krafft-Ebing (a key figure in the development of psychiatry) and John Harvey Kellogg (inventor of Corn Flakes and opponent of masturbation) considered the loss of semen to be physically and mentally debilitating (Terry 1999). They believed non-procreative sex drained men of vitality and caused effeminacy. Their work put a scientific gloss on medieval Christian views of gender in which the pleasure of "fornication" was believed to obscure rationality, making men first feminine and eventually less than human (Boswell 1980; Jordan 1997). The idea that there is a continuum of rationality with men at the top, women beneath them, and animals at the bottom can be found in a number of disciplines. Creating a continuum allows for the possibility of movement up or down the spectrum. Non-human animals are assumed to lack rational thinking and are least like the Christian God (implicitly present at the top of this ladder even in scientific manifestations of this thinking), while men are most God-like. Women are thought to be less rational than men and therefore are considered closer to animals. The God-like men 'naturally' rule the women and non-human animals. This approach, which equates women with nature, can be found in many European writings about "The New World," describing the territories as a woman to be sexually subdued (Robinson 2019 b).

Rich highlights the problems that gendering poses for women, whose gender position is constantly marking their enslavement to men. To reject gender supremacy, it seems to me that we must also reject the continuum of rationality these gender categories assume, which would require rejecting the speciesism that believes irrational animals are here for our use. I'm hesitant to scrap the continuum entirely, although I reject the idea that it's a hierarchy of rationality. In Mi'kmaw culture humans and other animals are on a continuum of being where shifting is possible. We have stories of humans who become other animals, non-humans who become human, and these stories usually don't frame us as the dominant species (Robinson 2014). If there is nothing degrading about being another type of animal then differences of human being (versus, say, rodent being or bird being) lose their meaning as markers of superiority. When we reject the basis for human domination of other animals, all power relations change.

## Monique Wittig's: *The Straight Mind*

It's difficult not to read postmodern deconstruction back onto earlier works—particularly in the case of Wittig—but I'll try. First published in 1980, the first step of Wittig's argument is that "man" and "woman" are political and economic categories rather than natural categories (making the essay pair nicely with Rich's argument). Wittig further argues that these categories mirror those of master and slave such that the enslaved category (woman) only makes sense in relation to the category of the master (men). Wittig's argument draws on the work of German philosopher Georg Wilhelm Friedrich Hegel over 170 years earlier (1977 [1807]) and cites French sociologist Colette Guillaumin's 1977 work on how racial categories are used to justify slavery. Wittig argues the oppression of women by men "produces the doctrine of the difference between the sexes to justify this oppression" (1992, p. 250). So it's not that women are different and therefore oppressed but that women are oppressed and therefore must be seen as different. To liberate ourselves from oppression, Wittig suggests, we need to escape the man/woman unit itself.

I tend to read Wittig's man/woman unit as describing in gendered terms the relationship that Rich names as compulsory heterosexuality, and I think such a relationship between gender and sexuality is implied in Wittig's essay itself:

> The refusal to become (or to remain) hetero-
> sexual always meant to refuse to become a man
> or a woman, consciously or not. For a lesbian
> this goes further than the refusal of the role

*"woman." It is the refusal of the economic, ideological, and political power of a man* (Wittig 1992, p. 248).

The possibility of escaping from the man/woman unit—and therefore escaping heterosexuality itself—raises more questions than the essay answers. Still, it offers intriguing hints: "To refuse to be a woman," Wittig writes, "does not mean one has to become a man" (1992, p. 247). Therefore, liberation isn't about shifting to the more dominant position in the dyad. One page later, Wittig describes the feminist and lesbian movement (presented in the singular in the English translation, suggesting it is the same) as fighting "for a sexless society" (1992, p. 248), which I take to mean a society without oppression (at least in terms of sex).

A society outside of categories of sex (which Wittig uses as synonymous with gender) is implied but not detailed in part because Wittig does not see much evidence of society existing outside of the man/woman unit. The only hint regarding what might be "outside" heterosexuality comes at the end of the essay:

*Lesbian is the only concept I know of which is beyond the categories of sex (woman and man), because the designated subject (lesbian) is not a woman, either economically, or politically, or ideologically. For what makes a woman is a specific social relation to a man, a relation that we have previously called servitude...a relation which lesbians escape by refusing to become or stay heterosexual* (Wittig 1992, p. 250).

If I follow Wittig's argument and agree that man/woman is a unit that comprises heterosexuality and that lesbians are not "for men" and therefore fall outside of the man/woman unit, then where do I stand as a bisexual? Bisexuality becomes a category of lesbian existence (if we escape being enslaved to men) or a one-foot-in-one-foot-out position in the compulsory heterosexual dynamic and therefore never fully free. Drawing on Mi'kmaw language, which speakers tell me is verb-based rather than noun-based, I speculate that the problem may be solved if we think of man, woman, lesbian, and bisexual as things people *do* rather than things people *are*. Those in the man/woman unit are not "naturally" men and women, but "people who man" and "people who woman." Similarly, those outside the unit have stopped "man-ing" or "woman-ing" and are now (in Wittig's words) lesbian-ing. I think this approach is in keeping with Hegel's own focus on the active nature of verbs related to being.

Wittig's work leads me to wonder what is "outside" of the compulsory instrumental carnism (the use and consumption of non-human animals) at the root of settler colonial culture. Where is the exit of settler carnism to escape hierarchies that dominate and use women, other animals, and Indigenous territory? Wittig suggests that to get outside heteropatriarchy, we must leave our position in gendered heterosexuality. According to Wittig, escaping enslavement to men requires shedding the identity (woman) that was the vessel for that relationship to power. Love between individuals of different genital configurations would be possible outside of heteropatriarchy, but it wouldn't be "straightness" as we know it. In a colonial context, I think Wittig is correct, but I don't think that analysis applies as easily to Indigenous cultures. Indigenous men have suffered heavily due to the difference between the settler masculinity foisted upon them and the traditional masculinites of many Indigenous nations. Pushing Wittig's argument further, one could stop man-ing and escape heteropatriarchy, and this might help us understand what is achieved by the masculinities some Indigenous men (particularly two-spirit men) have reclaimed.

## Tying It All into a Medicine Bundle

Connecting all this European theory to Indigenous health, I note that Indigenous scholarship takes a broad, holistic view of health. While some Indigenous health scholars focus on diseases and their causes and cures, many of us consider factors such as emotional balance, spiritual engagement, and good social relationships to be more significant for maintaining wellness. This is reflected in using the term "medicine" to describe anything that promotes wellbeing, such as dancing, singing, or socializing. If wellbeing is the result of specific social relationships (Hanrahan 2019) and gender is a way we relate to others (including other animals), then gender is a factor in how we achieve and maintain wellness by shaping how we interact with others.

In Indigenous circles, there's a movement away from the colonized diets and the health problems they cause. Some Indigenous people promote a return to traditional diets, sharing stories of physical and spiritual rejuvenation after abstaining from processed products. A *National Post* article, for example, shared the story of Bossy Ducharme, a Métis from Duck Bay, Manitoba, who "managed to drop to 145 pounds, without exercising (Calabrese 2012). Ducharme is quoted as saying, "I'm not going to put anything in my body that was not here before the Europeans arrived" (Calabrese 2012). Stories of individuals being "saved" by traditional diets can uncritically promote settler values around body size and overlook or sideline the importance of plant foods in favour of animals such as fish or elk, re-centering meat (Robinson 2019 b).

While I dislike arguments that use Indigenous people as evidence (usually to argue a practice or belief is older than dirt), the stereotypes applied to us help me understand patterns of gendering. Indigenous men are often presented as bow-hunting meat-eaters to support arguments about nature, masculinity, and meat-eating (Robinson & Corman, 2017). Noticing this stereotype helped me see a similar phenomenon in portrayals of settler men that combine sport, aggressive masculinity, and the heavy consumption of meat (e.g., nearly every Superbowl ad). Such gendering is similar to that of the degenerationalists mentioned above. Only instead of the loss of semen, it is the loss of meat that makes men effeminate and weak. In that argument masculinity is not inherent to being male but is an achievement that constantly requires "topping up" through defeating and consuming animals.

Building on the work of Rich and Wittig, I

wonder "What is outside of these binary systems?" whether the binary is straight/queer, man/woman, or human/non-human. If we go outside these binaries, what do we become? Rich and Wittig suggest there is something unpredictable or wild about the outside. As part of a nation that has been characterized as wild (in French *sauvage*) itself, that sounds rather appealing to me.

*Cited Works*

Ahmad, A. (2015, June 30). Feminism Beyond the Waves. *Briarpatch*. https://briarpatchmagazine.com /articles/view/feminism-beyond-the-waves

American Psychiatric Association (2013). *Diagnostic and Statistical Manual of Mental Disorders (DSM-5®)*. American Psychiatric Publishing.

Boswell, J. (1980). *Christianity, Social Tolerance and Homosexuality*. Chicago, IL: University of Chicago Press.

Butler, J. (1987). Variations on Sex and Gender: Beauvoir, Wittig, And Foucault. In *Feminism as Critique: On the Politics of Gender* (pp. 128-142). S. Benhabib and D. Cornell (Ed.). Minneapolis, MN: University of Minnesota Press.

Calabrese, D. (2012, May 18). Yes to berries, no to salt: Aboriginal man goes back to his dietary roots in order to lose weight, live healthier. *National Post*: https://nationalpost.com/news/yes-to-berries-no-to-salt-aboriginal-man-goes-back-to-his-dietary-roots-in-order-to-lose-weight-live-healthier

Dunn, R. (2012, July 23). Human Ancestors Were Nearly All Vegetarians. *Scientific American* Blog: https://blogs.scientificamerican.com/guest-blog/human-ancestors-were-nearly-all-vegetarians/

Government of Canada (2019). History of Canada's Food Guides: From 1942 to 2007. *Health Canada*. Ottawa, ON: https://www.canada.ca/content/dam/hc-sc/documents/services/food-nutrition/canada-food-guide/resources/evidence/food-nutrients-health-interim-evidence-update-2018/26-18-2165-History%20of%20CFG-EN-06.pdf

Guillaumin, C. (1988 [1977]). Race and Nature: The System of Marks. *Gender Issues*, 8(2), 25-43.

Hanrahan, C. (2019, Aug 22). Personal conversation.

Harrad, K. (2016). *Purple Prose: Bisexuality in Britain*. Portland, OR: Thorntree Press.

Hegel, G.W.F. (1977 [1807]). *Phenomenology of Spirit*. Translated by AV Miller. Oxford, UK: Clarendon Press.

Hughes, A. (2019, Feb 6). Indigenous representation in Canada's Food Guide. *Native America Calling:* http://www.nativeamericacalling.com/wednesday-february-6-2019-indigenous-representation-in-food-recommendations/

Jolson, L. (2018, Jan 17). Where's the beef? Industry stakeholders cry foul over Health Canada food guide freeze-out. *Hill Times*: https://www.hilltimes.com/2018/01/17/efforts-revamp-food-guide-lobbying-efforts-suggest-competing-departmental-priorities/131071

Jordan, P. (2001). *Neanderthal: Neanderthal Man and The Story Of Human Origins*. Cheltenham, UK: The History Press.

Jordan, M.D. (1997). *The Invention of Sodomy in Christian Tradition*. Chicago, IL: University of Chicago Press.

Kant, I. (2011[1873]). Rational Beings Alone Have Moral Worth. In *Food Ethics*, (pp. 10-12). P. Pojman and L.P. Pojman (Ed), Scarborough ON: Cengage

Learning.

McCue, D. (2019, Jan 27). This Indigenous scholar chose a vegan diet to honour Mi'kmaw teachings. *CBC Radio, Cross Country Checkup:* https://www.cbc.ca/radio/checkup/will-you-embrace-the-food-guide-s-plant-based-diet-1.4992293/this-indigenous-scholar-chose-a-vegan-diet-to-honour-mi-kmaw-teachings-1.4995159

McMillan, L. J. (2018). *Truth and Conviction: Donald Marshall Jr. and the Mi'kmaw Quest for Justice.* Vancouver, BC: UBC Press.

PETA (2015, Jan 17, 10:30am). Twitter post: https://twitter.com/peta/status/556519065112821760

Rich, A. (1980). Compulsory Heterosexuality and Lesbian Existence. *Signs: Journal of women in culture and society*, 5(4), 631-660.

Robinson, M. (2014). Animal Personhood in Mi'kmaq Perspective. *Societies*, 4(4), 672-688.

Robinson, M. (2019a). Two-Spirit Identity in A Time of Gender Fluidity. *Journal of Homosexuality* special Issue: What's in A Name?

Robinson, M. (2019b). The Big Colonial Bones of Indigenous North America's "Obesity Epidemic." *Thickening Fat: Fat Bodies, Intersectionality and Social Justice* (pp. 15-28). J. Rinaldi, M. Friedman, & C. Ride (Ed.). London, UK: Routledge.

Robinson, M. and Corman, L. (2017). All My Relations. In: *Animal Subjects 2.0: A New Ethical Reader in a Posthuman World*, pp. 229-248. J. Castricano & L. Corman (Ed.). Waterloo, ON: Wilfrid Laurier Press.

Sagan, A. (2019, Feb. 27). Dairy Farmers pull ad after complaints over alleged misleading the public. *National Post*: https://nationalpost.com/pmn/life-pmn/food-life-pmn/dairy-farmers-pull-ad-after-complaints-over-alleged-misleading-the-public

Smith, A. (2010). Queer Theory and Native Studies: The Heteronormativity of Settler Colonialism. *GLQ: A Journal of Lesbian and Gay Studies*, 16(1-2), 41-68.

Stanford, C.B. (1999). *The Hunting Apes: Meat Eating and The Origins of Human Behavior*. Princeton, NJ: Princeton University Press.

Terry, J. (1999). *An American Obsession: Science, Medicine and Homosexuality in Modern Society*.

Chicago, IL: University of Chicago Press.

United States Department of Agriculture (2011). *A Brief History of USDA Food Guides*: https://www.choosemyplate.gov/sites/default/files /relatedresources/ABriefHistoryOfUSDAFoodGuides .pdf

Weis, T. (2013). *The Ecological Hoofprint: The Global Burden of Industrial Livestock*. London, UK: Zed Books Ltd.

Wittig, M. (1992). *The Straight Mind and Other Essays*. Boston, MA: Beacon Press.

Wrangham, R. (2009). *Catching Fire: How Cooking Made Us Human*. New York, NY: Basic Books.

## *A Tale of Vermin*

Ikora Rey

I have mice in my home.

As a Black Queer person on a white island, I feel trapped like a mouse in a maze. I feel that I am being watched and judged and that my actions are constantly studied to be later applied to the rest of my community.

They bait me.

They catch me in traps and laugh while I cry out.

They don't see me as them.

They see me as vermin.

A study animal. A pest. A joke.

As my neighbors furiously shout, "kill them, kill the mice!" they have mockery in their eyes, as they think, "who would put the lives of mice over their own convenience?"

In their minds, they are meaningless. A joke. A pest. A vermin. A study animal —use them as a test to generalize all vermin.

"Let them die," they say without hesitation.

I tried the usual vinegar, peppermint, and cleanliness to keep the mice out. When they failed, I told my neighbors that I bought traps just to shut them up. They consoled weak little me saying "it's for the best dear. It has to be done..."

I did get traps — no-kill traps. I put the mouse's favorite snack inside them: my vegan red licorice. I waited until I heard the snap of the trap. I looked at the little one's eyes. They had their tail stuck in the door of the trap. Oh God, I'm sorry little one. I'm so sorry.

I see them see me, knowing they are being watched. They know they are small. They know I can crush them. They cower. They curl up. They cry. They look at me with a hesitation all too familiar. As I move the trap outside, the mouse cowers in fear. They curl up because they give up. They know their death is eminent. They know it's because of me.

I'm crying in my office. How does one not feel this pain for other beings? How does one not feel these emotions? Is it because one doesn't recognize the emotions? Is it that this mouse and I are kin? We know each other's pain. We both have the same pain. We're both trapped in a world where we are at the mercy of others that that don't see us as individuals. They don't recognize our differences are our strengths.

Today, little mouse, today we live. Together, we resist the same oppressive and deadly system that both connects and divides us.

FELIZ BRUECK AND McNEILL

## *Suffering from Oppression, We Oppress*

Janine Fuentes

My grandmother was someone I looked up to, someone who I thought should keep me safe. I was watching her from the window when I saw her wring a chicken by her neck. Stunned and disoriented, the chicken stumbled around on the ground with her neck broken, flapping her wings while screaming in agonizing pain until she eventually collapsed, calling out for help, a victim of a horrible murder.

I can't remember how old I was—maybe eight or 10, but that summer visiting my grandmother in Puerto Rico was a turning point in my life. Something changed inside of me. My cognitive dissonance was slowly growing into something I needed to acknowledge and address. What I saw didn't make sense. How could I be OK with something that was so horrific and done to another living being? The feelings I found myself struggling with were more than just a loss of innocence. It was an awakening—to the plight of other animals as well as my own. I learned later on in life that most people experience cognitive dissonance, meaning

153

we may have inconsistent thoughts or beliefs that they either ignore or decide to reconcile. After this experience, I began abstaining from eating the body parts of nonhuman animals. A turkey leg, a chicken wing, the body of a full fish, I couldn't stand the sight of anything on my plate that resembled a living being, let alone eat it. However, my family would try to persuade me; they would insist that humans had to eat other animals to survive. They attempted to reason that exploiting nonhuman animals, and especially eating them, was a necessary part of our diet and culture. They assured me that I would get sick if I did not consume them. So, I gave in and reluctantly, ate flesh in small amounts so long as they did not look like an animal.

However, my concern for the rights of other species only grew with age. I began to think about the interconnections of being someone whose free will, as a young lesbian, was disregarded in similar ways to the nonhuman animals that I watched strangers and my own family members brutalize. Their free will and the rights to their own bodies, expression, and rights were ignored. I saw myself in the nonhuman animals I met along the way. Like they were, in an unjust system dependent on oppressive hierarchies, I too felt the marginalization from those with power over me. A bird, a dog, or a horse do not have rights to their own lives in a society that punishes those that are different to what society expects us to be. I would eventually learn that I didn't have the right to pursue my own self-autonomy as a young girl attracted to other girls.

Hate and the pressures exerted by our community to conform, as well as my own suffering as I was forcibly separated from her, led my first love, Vanessa, to kill herself. The ridicule and abuse from friends, family, and most of society for being gay weighed too heavy on her. She was pulled out of school and isolated from everyone who cared about her, including me. I was moved three time zones away from her. I carried guilt the rest of my life, believing I could have done more to help her. After being snuck into her funeral, I realized that her sacrifice, giving up her life, had no impact on her family's hate for those who were different; these were church people. It was too late to save her, but I promised myself to do all I could going forward to help others that were abused, oppressed, used as well as murdered in any way I could. As my life moved forward, a sense of justice seeking continued to grow in me. I eventually became committed to working against the oppression of both human and nonhumans, and in 1994, I became vegan.

Like I was, children are often taught that they need to toughen up to survive. In our society, showing emotion, vulnerability, and standing firm against harm, consistently, is considered a weakness. However, I would argue that these may be some of the greatest strengths we can choose to embrace. Watching the chicken being killed made it clear that I knew killing (and what I later recognized as the oppression of those with less power) was wrong. This injustice that society had taught my grandmother was normal against other living beings transcended into unconsciously allowing other forms of harm to enter our home. It stops with me. As a gay vegan Woman of Color, I can say that I choose to act on ensuring normalized injustices do not continue in my name regardless of my upbringing, culture, or identity. I know it is my duty and privilege to help beings in need until my life ends.

## *First Vegan, Then Homo?*

Agnieszka Rahela Olszak

In Poland, it is not uncommon to hear insults shouted at someone because of their origin, race, sexuality, or even diet. One well-known saying, "First vegan, then homo," can be heard yelled out by those who consider themselves "true" men; however, most of them are just Nazis. That's correct – in the 21st century, we still have boys declaring themselves to be the defenders of their homeland.

This saying and description provides the backdrop to my personal story, but to tell you this story, I will need to start with how I was brought up.

I grew up in a family that recognized the Christian faith as something that should be practiced, or rather respected, because my parents didn't go to Church each Sunday, only on holidays.

I was also forced to do so but mostly because of the religion classes we took at school. I had to participate in a Rosary Circle; I even had to pass all the Christian subjects just to graduate from school. I didn't understand why I had to do it. It was something that just had to be done. Because of all this religious practice over a long period of time, I didn't allow myself to think that I could love a person of the same sex even though I already did. Instead, I explained to myself that it was just a high school friendship, and being a teenager meant I was full of overwhelming and uncontrolled emotions.

The emotions were so strong that after the end of my friendship (my friend found a boyfriend), I didn't understand what had happened, and I didn't want to live in the world. Today, in retrospect, I know that it was a terrible time that affects all of us in the LGBTQIA+ community. Only those who can count on the support of their family and friends and those who have the strength to struggle for years to learn to accept themselves will survive.

My family didn't know what was going on in my life at the time, and I couldn't understand these emotions either. I quickly returned to the "normality" that was expected of me. After all, I had so many "role models" around me, which were constant reminders of the path that my life was supposed to follow: "strong" men were meant to take care of their families as had been done from generation to generation. This included hunting and bringing back the corpses of nonhuman animals for the women. How could I break out of this pattern in which I was expected to become part of those unspoken traditions? I wasn't exactly forced to live like that, but I didn't even think that I could do it some other way. I just remember thinking "I cannot disappoint my family."

Everyone around me was heterosexual, and every family meeting reassured me that every relationship must follow an expected path. Every woman in my family was oppressed – used as a servant without a right to object.

This was fueled by the "King," my grandfather, who was the best hunter in the district and a decorated soldier. He was even awarded the actual title along with a crown for his hunting achievements. I remember the moments where he would tell us how to kill wolves if they somehow attacked us. I had a very difficult time respecting my grandfather, and I think it was ultimately because of him that I started to change myself – even against his rules. I didn't want to eat dead ducks on holidays; I wasn't happy that he killed all those nonhuman animals for us. I couldn't even have a dog of my own that wasn't a hunting dog. All the nonhuman animals I had adopted, those that had no purpose in hunting, tended to disappear in strange circumstances.

Following the expected path, at the age of 15, I called myself a straight girl even though I felt more like a boy because I spent most of my time with them. However, around this time, I stopped eating most meat dishes. I had reached a point where I had had enough of seeing dead rabbits on my grandmother's balcony waiting to be skinned. I had enough of touching "goose skin" on a chicken that had just been plucked. I had enough of all these cruel traditions forced on me by my family – the hypocritical image of God-fearing people pretending to have perfect marriages. When you looked at them from the outside, you might have thought they were happy. About 30 of us met every Christmas and ate around a table filled with dishes prepared by grandmother. Of course, every dish was made up from killed animals. However, after a few glasses of vodka, the worst started to come out – hard words, slander, and children ordered to go out to play in another room. It was only years later that I understood who was having an affair, who betrayed whom, and what has been an illusion. These perfect marriages existed only for show after Christmas and onwards.

The ham in the fridge seemed more and more disgusting to me (it was the '90s so not everyone could afford ham), so I gave the pork loin to the dog under the table. I gave the meat sandwiches to every nonhuman animal on the way back from school. I loved nonhuman animals, and I hated the fact that, in my family, they were made into trophies and killed without a thought.

I still remember the smell of hair from a pig's leg tanned over a burner in the house. The meat was a barter commodity since, in those days, people swapped sausages, pig's thighs, and tongue in exchange for services. Poland was a poor country, so meat was treated like gold and other animals were just objects. Growing up in these conditions, it was hard to shun all these gifts, and I couldn't oppose my family because I was afraid.

I was afraid of God (all those Christian lessons stayed with me for a long time). I was afraid of rejection and exclusion, so for a long time I pretended to be "normal." Then, at the age of 21, everything cracked like a snow globe with a perfect house inside.

Everything fell apart, but I stayed strong. I met my first girlfriend and felt so grown-up. I felt different and better. I had finally experienced something that made me happy, and I wanted to shout to the whole world that homosexuality is the best thing that can ever happen to a person. But then, I realized that I couldn't hold my girlfriend's hand in a public place; I couldn't kiss her on the street. When I opened up to the people I cared about, I realized even more that I couldn't live in the way I wanted. The friends, who I had grown up with and sat with at the same bench we had for the past ten years told me that I was "sick." They suddenly stopped being my friends. So, I was, once again, alone.

My mother insisted that she hadn't raised me well, and that "it" needed treatment. She couldn't know much about homosexuality as she was raised in a straight, traditional family. Psychologists at the time claimed that homosexuality was a disorder in itself and could be cured by electroshock "therapy." She thought that I was dysfunctional, whereas my two brothers where "normal." She stopped calling me, and for about two years, she only communicated with me to check if I was still alive.

I decided to accept that I was destined to be alone but with my girlfriend. I was supposedly finally free, and yet I was still in a cage. We were left to live and eat, but we were still controlled in every other aspect like a chicken or a pig in a factory farm. So, we could live yet only as was allowed by those in power. I could kiss my girl but only in our home. Affection in public was not allowed.

I became strong and weak at the same time. I found my identity, yet I lost my social status. I was happy and sad at once because I was excluded from my own family and the friends I had known.

Ten years later, everything fell apart for the second time. I found myself wondering if I was truly gay. My girlfriend had left me for a boyfriend, so I started wondering if maybe, in the end, we all end up with people from the opposite sex. During this time, my mother accepted me back, but she hoped that I would go back to "normal" since she thought it had all just been a prank.

In my search to understand myself once again, I started going to equality marches for the LGBT community. (That's how we called them in Poland at the time. It wasn't the same as Pride, however. At that time, there was no talk about trans people or asexual people.). I also started learning about women's history as well as the history of LGBT people. It was a damn difficult time where I struggled and felt injustice deeply. However, feminism had begun to become a part of me, and this was the time when I realized that the fight for nonhuman animal rights was similar to my own fight to be a free and independent woman – and lesbian.

I did not understand why women, especially the feminists I knew, ate meat. I know that it is a rarely debated subject in feminist circles in Poland perhaps because feminists are already often thought of in a bad light. They are stereotyped as women who hate all men, for instance, or they are all loud and hairy (which is fine for women to be, of course). In this sense, it would then appear, to me, that if they also start talking about animal rights, they may be ridiculed even further. This is perhaps the fear behind the silence, or maybe it is the desire to not be associated with sexist language as Carol J. Adams writes:

> *When a woman responds to mistreatment by protesting "I'm a human being!" or "I want to be treated with respect, not like some animal" what is she suggesting about the acceptable ways of treating other animals? Perhaps because comparison between women and nonhuman animal so often entail sexism, many women are anxious to distance themselves from other animals. Feminists, especially recognize that negative*

*'animal' imagery has advanced women's oppressions.*

So why it is not so common? Should we have feminists only for women's rights, animal activists only for animal rights? I know that is easier to focus on one issue at a time, but united we can do more for all of us. Similarly, many zero-waste pioneers care only about plastic and often ignore the fact that they can achieve more by changing their diets since fishing lines make up the majority of plastic waste in the oceans, for example. Therefore, by excluding fish from their plates, they can do more than excluding straws from their drinks. I couldn't stand the inability of movements unable to extend themselves beyond single issues, and my passion became ignited; I started to write a blog and read as much as I could. The books were mostly about animal rights and nonhuman animal feelings, but these topics led me to books like *Animals and Women* written by Adams and Josephine Donovan.

I remember the day before I finally went vegan very well: when I met a girl with whom I started to talk maturely about veganism. She was a woman whose sensitivity moved me. We started dating, and a year later, I deliberately gave up eating cheese, we excluded dairy products from our diet, and we started to support local organizations such as the Open Cages Association as volunteers. It's been seven years now since we have been vegan, a couple, and proud lesbians.

Still, at that time, we felt that nothing we did was enough. We wanted to give even more towards nonhuman animal liberation. We both had corporate jobs and earned a lot of money. This meant that we could spend large sums of money to help nonhumans, but even then, it was not enough.

I had been working in the fashion industry, and I had learned that my actions and employment contributed to the degradation of the environment. The planet doesn't need so many clothes and fast fashion or billions of chemicals used in denim production (and later discarded into the river.) After a trip to Bangladesh, I realized what the industry was doing to people in these countries even though they could in theory support the local community if they were ethical in their practices. However, their practices were destructive since many people had no alternative and were forced to work for clothes companies, which paid them a pittance.

I knew that thanks to my work I could support many organizations with my donations; I knew that despite all the evil, my career was giving work to people in Bangladesh, the only one that provided them with a stable livelihood. Bangladesh can only be understood when you are in Bangladesh. It is easy for those of us in the privileged Global North to shout to boycott large corporations; however, it is not easy to imagine how this boycott will affect millions of unemployed people in the poorest parts of Dhaka. This problem is not only a problem with large corporations but also with the government, including our own, which allows corporations to exploit countries and people in the Global South. Broken down by this all, I eventually could no longer continue with my work. It was then that I knew my 13 year-long career was over. I did not know what would happen next, but I knew that I had to break out of my comfort zone. I wanted to do something more, something good for this world.

So, I, an adult, a conscious vegan, a committed lesbian, blogger, activist and feminist, realized that I needed a change. I dreamt of working to help nonhuman animals in my country, so that became my goal. I took a chance, and it finally happened. I became an employee of Open Cages. My work for nonhuman animals has been an opportunity for me to continually grow, and I have felt safe to be my authentic queer self since. Giving back, at this point in my life, also includes supporting human rights issues financially since even one dollar can support someone that is experiencing poverty in the classist, capitalistic society that we live in. The most marginalized amongst us tend to be the most financially insecure. Donating is something we can all do for our community.

Thinking back to the beginning of my journey and the phrase "First vegan, then homo" and you know what? It's actually the perfect combination, but rather, in my case, it was "first homo, then vegan." We are homo – homo sapiens. We are animals. Nonhumans have voices. We just have to listen to them and to raise them. We should not compare our oppressions because they are not the same, however. Black, Indigenous, queer, trans, women, and nonhuman animals have rights, and we fight for them because the oppressors use the same tools against us all. No, we cannot compare our struggles, but we can unite in this fight for a better tomorrow.

## *Breaking Through*

Karla Galvez


My Guatemalan heritage is something I have always celebrated. I was confronted with racism when I wasn't even in grade school yet. As a child, you don't truly understand why people hate you for simply not being white and speaking more than one language. My father told me that people will always hate us for the color of our skin, our hair, our accents, our strong family ties, but he taught me to never be ashamed of who I am. I am constantly reminded of his words. I knew that my life would be difficult, but I also knew I could not live as being what others "expect" of me. Those expectations lied heavily in being heterosexual, married, and having kids. The culture in Utah (and the rest of the U.S., for that matter) is highly focused on those things, but it never made sense to me. While those are culturally accepted norms in white culture, this focus is also normalized in Latinx culture, too. The culture of most U.S. Americans is to work, "achieve," consume, debt, isolate, and repeat. While I find value in labor, it feels like joy and connection to those around you are often not prioritized in this cycle. To me, this promotes individualism, and it removes the importance of community through them. Early on, I knew my close connections to family and friends would keep me alive.

I began my involvement with activism in my early teen years. During this time of my life, I was fueled by anti-war/imperialism issues as well as LGBTQIA+ advocacy. I was a new high school student. George W. Bush began his "War on Terror" on Afghanistan and then Iraq. This was a disgusting act of imperialism and power, and I noticed how xenophobia was overt and how our Muslim friends were targeted. The school I was attending penalized me for sharing my views and challenging conservatives.

While I was aware of the racism that I confronted as a child, I also knew I was different in other ways. I knew that I wasn't only attracted to cis men — women were much more than just "inspiring" to me. At the same time, I also didn't understand being misgendered so much. I was often asked "Are you a boy or a girl?" and I couldn't answer because I didn't feel I fit either label. This is where my queer identity began, as a child, despite my not having the language to express it. Through this, I became aware of oppression and how others did not have these societal barriers.

In my youth, I also became fascinated with religions since I was raised Catholic, and it seemed like my own church didn't want me around for who I was and am. The Catholic church had a strong stance on homosexuality. Oh, how those who followed the teachings demonized those who were different. The things they spoke about just didn't make sense to me either. I studied the Bible due to my upbringing and found that maybe people didn't really read it after all. I eventually found the gem of Buddhism and quite frankly became infatuated with it. The theme of non-violence, compassion, and service to others that was part of this new religion made the most sense to me. I developed a love of philosophy and studied to find answers of who and what humans are supposed to be about. These were humble beginnings of questioning authorities, dogmas, and social norms.

As painful as it was to experience pure hate, violence, bullying, overt and covert racism, systemic oppression, degradation from others, Buddhism and my search for answers opened something in me. This path and what I learned opened the gift of empathy in me. I never wanted others to feel or be treated like I had been. How could I continue this in life when others didn't want me to be seen or live? I read more, studied more, and tried to find community.

I don't think people of privilege can relate that even in your own communities it can be isolating when you question and choose to live authentically. It was painful to have those like you leave you out as well. This left me questioning myself for some time: Where do I go? Can I be vulnerable? Will I burn out sharing who I am? Can I keep going? Am I just a dreamer? Fortunately, I was blessed to have a supportive family and friends who at times didn't get me but wanted me to live as I am. I wasn't bitter towards the Latinx community that didn't get me. I could see how we all faced the trauma of racism and colonization but wondered how sexual orientation and gender identity were so removed. I then learned about the connections of colonization and the rise of transphobia, for example. It is now known that trans folks existed before the colonization of the Western part of the world. People became homogenized and demonized for differences, so they become easier to control and to shame. In the end, colonization forcibly removed people that were a precious part of our community. I hoped that other Latinx would eventually open their minds and hearts to realize this all. At this point, I became committed to reducing suffering in any way I could and still can.

As life went on, I found communities outside the one I had grown up in that understood me including my love of other animals, which has always been a part of me. From a young age, at times, I found myself questioning what was at the dinner table and why it was considered a tradition. I often wondered, "What was the cost of this all?" In my anti-oppression stance and my commitment to the least harm, veganism was a path that I now see was inevitable. I have had companion animals since childhood, and one day, I stared deeply into my cat's eyes and thought, "How could anyone want to eat you or another living, breathing, feeling being?" I thought about the animals exploited and killed in violence for tradition, and it finally clicked. With tears in my eyes, I hugged my cat, and from then on, I transitioned from vegetarian to vegan.

I have privileges, and I try my hardest to raise the voices of the unheard and forgotten. To me, the systems of oppression are all connected. Capitalism drives companies to spend fortunes on studying the psychology of marketing, selling, and commodification. They make it so simple to detach us from what we buy to what we eat and erase those most affected by it – both nonhumans and marginalized humans. In the U.S., I think most can agree that violence towards domesticated animals (cats, dogs, etc.) is horrendous, and they should be protected by the law against any abuse. Yet, despite this common understanding and agreement, our society still limits this protection, which does not extend to domesticated nonhuman animals. Companies that kill nonhuman animals have changed the way you perceive them through the re-branding as living beings into things such as reducing chickens to nuggets or poultry, renaming cows to burgers or beef, and reducing fish into sticks or fillets. Doing this desensitizes people from what they are consuming and justifies the commodification of other animals as mere products for the taking. In essence, violence against other species is purposely normalized.

In saying that, mainstream white veganism forgets that cruelty-free does not exist. Who grows your food? Who picks your food? Who does the heavy work at the price of unfair and unethical labor? Food justice includes nonhuman beings *and* human beings.

There is a lot of deprogramming that happens when we are faced with the reality that nonhuman animal suffering does lead to human suffering. This deprogramming can look like questioning where your information comes from, reading content from voices that are usually not given a platform, and asking others why they do the things that they do or believe the things they do if they are new concepts for you. This is not a comfortable position to be in, but I find it is where we can start to make connections that we have been purposely taught to be unaware of. This can then transform to real change within our community and pass on to others.

As a Queer Brown person, when I started questioning and going beyond the mainstream norms, I eventually realized that embracing nonhuman animal rights meant fighting for others — and myself. It's not an either/or. We can work on the liberation of humans and nonhumans simultaneously. We can rally against the ICE agencies who are doing horrendous acts to families *and* adopt plant-based diets as well as choose to forgo things like products tested on animals, for example. We are all more than single-issue advocates. Veganism without support of human rights will never make sense to me. And, while the world of LGBTQIA+ people has made some strides, we have much to do still. I cannot pretend to not see the injustices our fellow humans and nonhuman animals constantly face. Because of this, I use my voice and actions to the best of my ability to show others how we can find compassion for all beings.

I chose to share my deeply personal story to help others make connections of the oppressive systems that may seem far apart but truly are not. Power is all around us. When we are faced with poverty, food deserts, racism, sexism, speciesism, ableism, homophobia, and transphobia, it can make it difficult to want to continue the fight for liberation of these systems, particularly if we may have privileges in one community and not the other. The Latinx/Guatemalan community is something I hold deep in my heart because it was the beginning of understanding who I am and what changes need to be done. I have since found that existing with all my intersections is to have a radical existence.

My radical existence and understanding mean that the days of being silenced and making the majority comfortable are over. I have seen how refusing to be complicit tests the character of folks — even those you thought were your friends or allies. Yet, it is possible to do so much through consistent actions as simple as speaking up to stop an ignorant comment. All it takes is a commitment to refuse to stay silent. Even more important is making choices based on the acknowledgment of the privileges we have other others and taking accountability when we are called to do so.

As for what comes next, I am only just getting started. *Por que siempre voy a ser chingonx.*

## *One White Queer's Thoughts on the Animal Welfare Movement*

Anonymous

I grew up in a family that prioritized making the world a better place. I was told to be a leader, an activist, a public servant, a humanitarian, or all of that bundled together. I was taught to care. I was pushed to empathize. I was trained to fight for a more ethical world.

For me, this translated to not stepping on worms when it rained, talking to trees as a child, and walking in the steps of my parents who were ecofeminists. When I was 11, I stopped eating meat. When I was 12, I refused to dissect a frog and spread around a petition that ended the use of apples being used as bait for deer in the backyard of our principal, an avid hunter. When I was 14, I went vegan and started organizing animal rights outreach. When I was 16, I went to an environmental youth leadership camp and was trained how to connect anti-speciesism to environmentalism, to labor rights, to feminism, to anti-colonialism.

I believe in justice that is consistent in its anti-oppression approach across movements. I'm not perfect, but I come from a positionality of whiteness. I live as an Irish-Scots settler in the Mountains. And sometimes, trying just isn't enough. I've worked in humanitarian organizations and animal welfare-NGOs since I was 18, and I've learned how to survive on minimum wage to fight for the world I believe in. I am a white "other." I suffer chronic pain and brain damage, I'm genderfluidflux, I'm neurodivergent, and I'm broke. However, none of that equals the systemic violence faced by Black Brown Indigenous People of Color. A trans ACLU staff attorney, Chase Strangio, wrote in the *Progressive (2019),*

> *None of these various struggles as I experience them, however, change the fact that I am white and trans. And the attacks on my body—individual and systemic—have not taken and could not take away the many ways that I am aligned with power.*

When I was working with the animal welfare group in 2018, I was told that the organization was wary of the Blue Wave. Thar organization was monetarily supporting Republican candidates be-cause they were "on our side" with the animal issues. When our "friendly" Republicans lost their race, there was a deep disappointment in our office.

In 2019, as I was interning for another welfare group, I walked out of a meeting. We were brainstorming about whether or not to support anti-CAFO measures in three states. My coworkers were nervous about alienating their Republican stake-holders in red states after spending years building tenuous relationships with these individuals. One co-worker mentioned that a messaging angle we could use to not alienate these legislators/Re-publican allies would be jobs. This white woman continued, saying that we could take advantage of the current discourse and politics of fear surround-ding immigration, the "rise of the East," and encroa-ching foreign powers on American soil. Of the 20 or so of us on the call, 18 of us were white.

In researching the tactic of using white supremacy in the suffrage movement and in the LGBT movement, I learned that social movements often recognize that *whiteness* trumps everything and is the true unifier. No matter what policy you are pushing, if it is wrapped in white supremacy, then it will win in racist United States of America.

Both of these groups that I've worked for are following the same old trick as the suffragettes—

utilize systemic violence against Black Brown Indigenous People of Color and wait for the results.[15] These groups have proven what so many vegan Voices of Color have already known, and I have always naively (and politically decided) to ignore—mainstream veganism is white supremacy.[16] These groups are not fighting the rise of fascism and the far-right but using this turn for their advantage. These groups are not disowning hate crimes—they are encouraging them.

I am almost a 10-year vegan, and I am nauseous writing these words. I've spent 12 years of my life trying to get y'all to go vegan for the environment, for the animals, and for your health. I don't need you all to have another excuse to be anti-vegan. I usually argue that I was bullied more in school for being vegan than being queer. But the vegan movement has been a limb of power being used to oppress Black Brown Indigenous People of Color.

The most mainstream animal rights and welfare organization in the US right now are pro-corporation and capitalism, have a violent posi-

---

[15]See *The Ideas of the Woman Suffrage Movement, 1890-1920* by Aileen Kraditor

[16]See Iman Chantila's capstone on "Veganism through a Racial Lens: Vegans of Color Navigating Mainstream Vegan Networks," or the wonderful Vegans of Color anthologies edited by Julia Feliz Brueck from Sanctuary Publishers.

tionality of whiteness, and have been touched by the #MeToo movement. I was personally affect-ted by that last point as I was sexually assaulted while canvassing for work. The organization I was volunteering with had a toxic workplace that put us in unsafe positions and environments. If we didn't participate or brought up our safety concerns, we were socially ostracized for "not doing enough."

We need to listen and give space to vegan Voices of Color, Afro-vegans, and Indigenous anti-speciesists.[17] We need to support labor, low-income, and anti-racist movements that might not center, or touch on, veganism at all.

I am a heartfelt believer that, if you can fight speciesism, you should include it in your repertoire of activisms. I am exhausted by the vegan hatred in my activist communities. We want to believe that if we are fighting for X, then we are not propagating violence against Y, but that's not how it works. I wish my LGBTQIA+ non-vegan friends would recognize that fighting for LGBTQIA+ rights but ignoring speciesism only aligns us with the oppressor. However, being vegan does not release

---

[17]Give your money to and uplift great groups like Sanctuary Publishers, Queer Nature, Sistah Vegan Project, and Black Vegans Rock.

you from fucking human decency. Animal welfare groups need to include anti-capitalism, anti-racism, and anti-misogyny in their priorities, otherwise you're just another group actively relying on white supremacy to protect and sustain you.

## *Toward an Anti-Carceral Queer Veganism*

Leah Kirts

As a white queer person from a conservative working-class farming and hunting community in the Midwest, my relationship with veganism was involuntarily queered and politicized from the beginning. When I became a vegetarian in my mid-20s, I received homophobic comments and right-wing political mockery from friends and family for my refusal to eat flesh. I was not yet out as a bisexual (and am still not fully out to many of these family members), but they unknowingly prompted me to examine what Carol J. Adams aptly defines as *The Sexual Politics of Meat* (1990), which offers an analysis of the heterosexist misogyny bound up in nonhuman animal consumption and patriarchal dominion. It was through the work of leftists like Black lesbian feminist Audre Lorde, queer ecofeminist Greta Gaard, and queer theorists Judith Butler and Sara Ahmed that my queerness and veganism began to evolve in tandem (Kirts 2018) as did my awareness of their roles as movements in part of a broader struggle against oppressive hierarchies like white supremacy and capitalism.

Black radical vegan scholars such as Dr. A. Breeze Harper, Aph & Syl Ko, and Christopher Sebastian McJetters write deftly about the historical relationship between white supremacy and speciesism (the belief in a human-animal binary where humans are superior). In reading their scholarship, I recognized my own ignorance of and complicity in the rhetoric of the nonhuman animal rights and gay rights movements that elevates the experiences of white cis men and white cis women who often reside a comfortable distance from the state-sanctioned violence of policing and incarceration. In and outside of liberal vegan activist circles, there is a strong presence of carceral politics (a reliance upon the correctional system also known as the penal system) to solve social problems by incarcerating individuals for hate crimes and nonhuman animal cruelty. Queer history is grounded in the Stonewall rebellion against police raids and against the routine violence and imprisonment of LGBTQ people; therefore, any political stance that upholds punitive justice (the belief that punishment can change behavior) is incompatible with queer politics but is especially antithetical to vegan principles. How could one demand the liberation of imprisoned nonhuman animals while simultaneously celebrating the imprisonment of humans?

There is a general lack of imagination within mainstream nonhuman animal advocacy about the plight of farm and slaughterhouse employees, and the recurrent criminalization of workers by carceral vegan activists stands out as a racial and class-based disconnect with the harsh realities of labor conditions in farming operations, something that I saw firsthand as an adolescent while helping on my uncle's dairy farm. In retrospect, I've grappled with my uncle's mistreatment of the dairy cows on his farm and how it mirrored his abuse and exploitation of the undocumented Mexican immigrants he employed for years in what can only be described as a form of indentured servitude.

By using a queer vegan anticapitalist and anti-carceral political framework, we can look at the institutional treatment of nonhuman animals and the mass incarceration of marginalized groups not as separate issues but as linked systems of oppression. The punitive justice system, animal agriculture and mainstream animal advocacy don't exist in political vacuums but are deeply connected. Similarly, radical liberation movements are also in dialogue with each other, sharing strategies, crossing borders, and overlapping efforts. It's crucial to think of veganism not as an end unto itself but as inseparable from other political movements striving for the total liberation of all marginalized bodies such as prison abolition, Black Power, queer and trans liberation, Indigenous land rights, the labor movement, and environmental justice.

In 2012, a poultry worker at a Butterball turkey farm in North Carolina became the first person in U.S. history to be convicted of a felony for cruelty to factory farmed birds. The arrest followed an undercover investigation by a prominent vegan animal advocacy group that led to the employee's sentencing, probation, fines, and subjection to warrantless searches by law enforcement (Borlick, 2012). Butterball management and executives weren't charged or fined for creating the conditions that led to the abuse of turkeys on the farm while the farm worker's arraignment was hailed as a milestone in the vegan movement. This would become an important legal precedent that would make future convictions of cruelty against farmed animals easier to secure (Runkle, 2012). According to local news, within six months, four more Butterball workers from the same farm were convicted of felonies (WECT News, 2013).

When advocates of nonhuman animals[18] champion the use of punitive justice, and more

---

[18]While there are distinct groups within the nonhuman animal movement, the central ideologies are animal rights, farmed animal protection, animal liberation, and animal welfare. In

specifically, when a white gay-led animal advocacy group chooses to align their work with the power of the American carceral system, such as in the Butterball case, it alienates and harms Black, Brown, Indigenous people of color (BBIPoC), lesbian, gay, bisexual, trans, queer (LGBTQ), and low-income communities that have historically been and continue to be targeted, harassed, detained, imprisoned, deported, and killed by the U.S. government at disproportionate rates (Dolovich 2011; Lambda Legal 2012; Hinton 2016). The instance of law enforcement punishing individuals for animal cruelty isn't evidence that the legal system is compassionate toward nonhuman animals. What is evident is that animal protection laws can and will be used to incarcerate individuals, and that is something that should alarm vegan animal advocates. Hence, the carceral state doesn't need to be veganized; it needs to be dismantled. My criticism of carceral veganism isn't meant to discredit the work of nonhuman animal liberation but to examine the interconnections of veganism with other social justice issues that also form part of discussion in other movements. This examination is valuable because it is foundational to achieving

this piece, I use the term animal advocacy to encompass the different facets of the movement without diminishing their distinctions. I also recognize that not all animal advocates are vegan and not all vegans are animal advocates.

liberation not only for nonhuman animals, but for all marginalized communities.

## Liberty and Justice for Whom?

In order to establish an anti-carceral queer vegan politics, it's necessary to first examine the roots of the U.S. carceral system. According to crime historian Dr. Gary Potter, American society operates under a centralized punitive justice system, the enforcement of which evolved out of an informal communal watch system in Northern cities during the mid-1600s and slave patrols in Southern states circa the early 1700s, that gained power in the mid-1800s as cities grew to absorb industrial labor while municipal forces grew to protect the interests of the economic elite, maintain civil order, and suppress the collective organizing power of the poor and formerly-enslaved (Potter 2013).

Northern police forces did the bidding of wealthy merchants, targeting the poor and working classes and disrupting organized labor strikes. Described by Potter as "paramilitary forces occupying the streets," municipal police departments stood between property-holding elite and "propertyless masses" deemed a "politically dangerous class" (Potter, 7). Although queer people are not named in Potter's research, given the criminality of homosexuality and gender noncomformity, we can be certain that queer people were among those whose behavior and movement was policed. Policing in the Southern colonies consisted of vigilante slave patrols that quelled slave revolts through methods of organized terror. After the Civil War, slave patrols evolved into police departments that enforced Jim Crow segregation laws and controlled the movement of formerly enslaved African Americans who labored in the U.S. agricultural caste system (Potter, 3).

Since its inception, policing in the U.S. has been used to enforce the white supremacist, cishetero, capitalist, and patriarchal agenda within society to protect the property of the rich, to maintain the status quo set by those who hold power, and to criminalize people who do not comply (Ritchie 2017). Punitive justice heavily informs how we interact in our communities today and how we respond to conflict both as individuals and as a society. Punishment isn't necessarily based on one's actions but is determined largely by one's perceived value in society, and U.S. society consistently upholds a hierarchy that privileges whiteness, wealth, heterosexuality, and cis-masculinity (Peterson 2012). This agenda has been and continues to be especially violent toward queer and trans BBIPoC through racial profiling coupled with gender policing by law enforcement (Springate 2016). People who occupy public space like homeless queer youth and trans sex workers are even more vulnerable to police brutality and arrest.

In contrast to punitive justice, prison abolition and restorative justice pose alternatives to the penal system that seek to repair the harm that has been caused to victims, offenders, and their communities through rehabilitation, reconciliation, and restoration. They seek to transform the extent to which federal and local governments are able to define and respond to crime (The Centre for Restorative Justice 2020). Nonviolent frameworks like restorative justice hold the individual responsible for their actions while engaging community accountability and teaching strategies for how to resolve conflict without involving the cops. The scope of restorative justice goes beyond mediating individual crimes and examines how socioeconomic factors like affordable housing, education, food security, and fair wages can reduce future crimes.

Angela Davis, a scholar, leader of the Black Power movement, political organizer, prison abolitionist, and lesbian vegan, illuminates the ways in which incarceration reinforces cycles of capitalist dispossession and perpetuates ideologies of ableism, speciesism, and heteropatriarchal white supremacy. In the early 1970s, Davis was targeted by the FBI after being labeled a dangerous terrorist by President Nixon. She was apprehended and held on bail for 16 months, some amount of which was spent in the New York Women's House of Detention in Greenwich Village while she faced the death penalty. House of D, the prison's informal title, was known for its high incarceration rates of lesbians and nonbinary people and thus became a queer meeting place for their lovers and friends on the outside (Ryan 2019). It was an important site of queer history and no coincidence that after fighting to be released from solitary confinement there, Davis began organizing from behind bars for her and others' release. Prison conditions were such that maggots infested the meat being served as food, prompting Davis to become a vegetarian and later begin to examine the relationship between the commodification of nonhuman animals and the marginalization of Black and Brown communities under capitalism.

In her recent book, *Freedom is a Constant Struggle* (2016), Davis explains how neoliberalism (a political economic model based on individualism, deregulated free market trade, and defunded social welfare protections) steers our focus toward individual victims and individual perpetrators causing us to believe that by exacting revenge on one person, we can eradicate a social problem. "By focusing on the individual as if the individual were an aberration," she writes, "we inadvertently engage in the process of reproducing the very violence that we assume we are contesting" (Davis 103). What this means is that laws that target discrimination and hate crimes encourage us to think about oppression in terms of individual action rather than the widespread failure of social welfare services.

With laws focused on personal bias and individual intent, the penal system is freed from having to account for the unequal distribution of wealth and social services like affordable housing, quality education, healthcare, and living wages. When these services are accessible to the public, crime rates are shown to drop (Dumont 2012). Incarceration does not solve for social deficits but exacerbates them by incurring tremendous emotional and financial burdens for inmates and their families on the outside. "Prisons do not disappear problems, they disappear human beings" (Davis 1998), extracting resources from communities through fines, court costs, bail bonds, telephone calls, and a lack of provisions behind bars, as well as the cost of extracting people from their communities (Wagner 2017). Abolition and restorative justice, however, are models that get at the root of crime and reduce recidivism (Ascione 2001). When locking someone away for causing harm to themselves or others is no longer an option, treatment, rehabilitation, and social accountability become mandatory responses. Offenses like nonhuman animal abuse can be processed through community-based programs where offenders and their families join with animal protection agencies and affected community members to collectively decide what holistic amelioration requires (Muller-Harris 2001).

## Industries Built on Exploitation

The lives of farm workers, imprisoned people, and nonhuman farmed animals are significantly different, yet it is important to iterate that the industries that exploit them operate in similar ways and are historically connected. Animal advocates and prison abolitionists share a similar goal: to empty cages. But prison abolition seeks more than to free prisoners from their cells but to render the entire system of incarceration obsolete. In many cases, nonhuman animal advocacy campaigns become tools that strengthen the arm of the carceral state rather than weaken it. Unlike dogs and cats, farmed animals are rarely set free after undercover investigations reveal their mistreatment nor do their conditions improve because a worker has been convicted of abuse. The laws, however, especially those that carry felonies, lead to the criminalization of individuals who often represent the most marginalized populations of low-wage workers in the country that experiences the most extreme and routine workplace exploitation and abuse (Sokol 2016).

Laws that protect nonhuman animals rarely include farmed animals because abuse is standard practice in hatcheries, on farms, and in slaughterhouses. Male chicks are macerated, females are forcibly inseminated, birds' beaks are clipped, piglets' tails are docked and testes ripped out without anesthesia, calves are separated from their mothers hours after birth, and slaughter lines operate at such high speeds that many animals are scalded and skinned while still alive (Solotaroff 2013). The legal and ceaseless confinement of nonhuman animals under industry practices varies state by state due to recent bans, but the majority of states still includes battery cages that are roughly the size of a sheet of paper where laying hens are crowded so tightly they're unable to spread their wings, gestation crates that pen sows in so tightly they cannot stand or turn around, veal crates, and tethering practices that restrict the movements of calves so they are unable to fully extend their limbs (Pachirat 2013).

Industrially farmed animals are born into such grotesquely unnatural conditions of confinement and treated with such calloused disposability that "disabilities become common, even inevitable," writes disabilities scholar and artist Sunaura Taylor in *Beasts of Burden: Animal and Disability Liberation* (2017). The disabilities caused by their toxic surroundings are "often secondary to the ones they are made to have from birth," writes Taylor. "Farmed animals are bred to extremes: udders produce too much milk for a cow's body to hold, turkeys and chickens cannot bear the weight of their own giant breasts, and pigs' legs are too weak to support them," Taylor continues (31). The genetic manipulation of farmed animals to produce more fluids and flesh than their bodies are able to produce results in their constant chronic pain, emotional distress, and mental illness.

Normalized violence against farmed animals pushes nonhuman animal advocacy groups to document what's considered unusual cruelty: behaviors that register as torturous to law enforcement because they're expressions of workers' personal desensitization, anger, stress, or sadistic humor and aren't industry practices nor directly tied to productivity. Advocacy groups create campaigns based on shocking undercover footage to lobby lawmakers and pressure law enforcement to act. A felony conviction is a marker of a successful campaign.

Nonhuman animal cruelty is a felony at the state level nationwide and a recent bill, the Preventing Animal Cruelty and Torture (PACT) Act, passed in 2019 making it a federal felony to kill nonhuman animals for entertainment (Deutsch 2013). However, the federal government simultaneously enforces the Animal Enterprise Terrorism Act, a bill passed in 2006 that criminalizes interference with nonhuman animal enterprises as an act of terrorism. Sentencing under the act can carry one year to life in prison (AETA, 2013). Under the same system, a person can be tried as a felon for mistreating nonhuman animals in ways that are unprofitable to the industry while another person can be tried as a terrorist for plotting to rescue nonhuman animals from being mistreated, which is also unprofitable to industry. The commonality between the two pieces of legislation is that they both protect the interests and profits of private property owners through the criminalization of workers and activists.

Moreover, industries based on the exploitation of nonhuman animals are notoriously awful places for workers because both lives have been devalued to the point of disposability for the sake of profit. The majority of the 250,000 poultry workers in the U.S. today are Black and Brown, immigrants, refugees, imprisoned people, and half are women (Sokol, 1). Across the largest American meat companies like Butterball, employees work grueling hours in dangerous conditions for poverty-level wages that average $27,790 per year (Bureau of Labor 2018).

The meat industry slaughtered 9 billion land animals in 2018 (over 20 million each day), the vast majority of whom were chickens (USDA 2019). In order to keep up with that scale of production, poultry workers are routinely denied bathroom breaks (Sokol, 10) and experience sexual harassment and threats of termination or deportation for complaining about their work conditions, requesting time off, and seeking medical aid for workplace injuries (Sokol, 30). They suffer from some of the highest rates of workplace PTSD in the U.S. as well as chronic pain and musculoskeletal disorders that lead to severe long-term medical injuries (Sokol, 7-9). They are five times more likely to become sick due to their occupation, three times more likely to have a limb amputated, and, due to the repetitive motions required to perform their jobs, seven times more likely to develop carpal tunnel than the national average (USDOL 2013). In its demand for ever-increasing profits, industrialized animal agriculture manufactures human and animal disability and largely gets away with it by hiring a workforce that cannot easily advocate for itself due to being social marginalized, economically impoverished, and politically criminalized; nonetheless, the turnover rate for an average meatpacking plant is 100 percent each year (Taylor, 185).

The poultry industry has a particularly long history of racism and suppression of workers who organize to demand fair wages and better treatment (Stuesse 2016), but it isn't unique from other industrial animal-based companies in that they all hold tremendous economic and political sway in their respective localities that's amplified by race, gender, and class privilege. Last year, the single largest ICE raid in U.S. history took place at a poultry processing facility in Mississippi during which nearly 700 Latin American employees were arrested and fired from their jobs. Many of the workers were members of the United Food and Commercial Workers Union, had been actively organizing for better wages and working conditions, and had recently won a $3.75 million-dollar sexual harassment settlement against one of the farms (Kirts 2019).

Another example of the monopolization of political and economic power is Fair Oaks Farm in Indiana, the fifth largest dairy cooperative in the U.S. that is considered to be the Disneyland of agritourism and a leader of sustainability in the dairy industry. In 2019, an undercover investigation carried out by the Animal Recovery Mission (ARM), a militarized nonhuman animal defense organization, revealed the routine abuse of calves and dairy cows by farm employees (Riess 2019). ARM prides itself on working with law enforcement agencies including the FBI, CIA, and ICE to conduct raids and facilitate the arrests of people engaged in unlawful acts of nonhuman animal cruelty (Elejalde-Ruiz 2019).

All of the Fair Oaks farm workers depicted harming calves were fired, but only one person was arrested: a 36-year-old undocumented immigrant from Mexico who was held on bond for misdemeanor and felony charges. When his undocumented status was discovered, local officials transferred him into ICE custody where he faced deportation (Bangert 2019). It's no coincidence that Fair Oaks' founder Mike McCloskey served on Trump's agricultural advisory committee on immigration reform (DelReal 2016). McCloskey's business benefits from the delegitimization of immigrants that his political efforts seek to uphold, and the undocumented worker's charges gave the illusion that justice was served in the face of bad press. After an event like this, it's common that undercover footage like ARM's is gathered and released to the public in order haunt viewers, inspire them to adopt vegan principles, boycott companies where animal abuse occurs, and donate money to fund more investigations. Rather than take an additional step to connect the abuse of nonhuman animals and workers in animal agriculture, the plight of the latter is almost always obscured.

There are salient connections between farming operations like Fair Oaks and other carceral systems. Beyond the physical similarities of metal gates, bars, locks and chains is a deep-rooted belief system that justifies the treatment of carceral subjects. In her book *Carceral Space, Prisoners and Animals* (2018), critical feminist scholar Karen Morin uses carceral geographies and critical animal studies to develop a "trans-species carceral geography" that identifies social and spatial relationships shared between imprisoned humans and nonhuman animals in sites of mirrored confinement and labor exploitation: death row and slaughterhouses, pharmaceutical testing laboratories and prison labor, zoos and solitary confinement. The proximity of humans to nonhuman animals contributes to the former being seen as "bestial" thereby making their treatment appear warranted.

Central to speciesism is an ableist assertion that vulnerability and dependency are undignified and reduce one's value. To be dependent is seen as an "inherently bad, even unnatural," characteristic among humans which "is played out across the species divide" (Taylor, 214). Taylor looks at the ways disabled people and domesticated animals are "presented as beasts and as burdens" in society, which holds relevance when we extend that scrutiny to the marginalization of incarcerated bodies. In the Stanford Prison Experiment, the perception of dependency was a determining factor in how people in the study assigned as guards responded to the people in the study assigned as inmates. McLeod writes, "As the prisoners became more dependent, the guards became more derisive towards them. They held the prisoners in contempt and let the prisoners know it. As the guards' contempt for them grew, the prisoners became more submissive. As the prisoners became more submissive, the guards became more aggressive and assertive" (2018).

Though an experiment, the behavior exhibited by the guards in the study closely mirrors the abuse of power that occurs through the arm of the state on a daily basis. The prison industrial complex (PIC) is a mass incarceration system that extends beyond federal and state prisons, and includes county jails, immigration and youth detention centers, military prisons, psychiatric hospitals, and holding cells. The carceral state systematically extracts resources from families of loved ones in the criminal justice system to fund its own governance in what is considered by scholars to be an "inversion of welfare for the poor" where the poor are funding the very system that imprisons them, the effects of which are cyclical and damaging (Katzenstein 2015). Whether or not individuals get convicted of the crimes they are charged with, their arrests lead to exorbitant bail bonds, pretrial detention, and commissary fees. Any amount of time spent behind bars, no matter how short, erodes wealth, perpetuates debt, and impedes future employment opportunities upon their release (Prison Policy Initiative 2019).

The U.S. has the highest incarceration rate in the world—655 out of 100,000 Americans are prisoners—with nearly 2.2 million incarcerated people as of 2016 (Kaeble & Cowhig 2018). According to the Prison Policy Initiative (PPI), the majority of inmates are confined in state prisons followed by local jails, the latter of which only 24 percent have been convicted of a crime (Sawyer & Wagner 2019). PPI reports that nearly half a million people (one in five imprisoned people) are incarcerated for non-violent drug offenses on any given day. Black people experience incarceration at six times the rate of whites while Latinx people are twice as likely to be imprisoned, and prisoners of all backgrounds are overwhelmingly from low-income communities when compared to the total U.S. population (PPI 2019).

Gays, lesbians, and bisexuals are incarcerated at three times the rate of the general population according to a study on incarceration rates of sexual minorities, the first of its kind, published by the American Public Health Association (Meyer et al. 2017). Broken down by group, the study reveals that gay men represent 9.3 percent of men in prison and 6.2 percent of men in jail whereas lesbian and bisexual women make up a staggering 42.1 percent of women in prison and 35.7 percent of women in jail. Trans people were not accounted for in this study, but according to Lambda Legal, in the U.S. nearly one in six trans or nonbinary people has been imprisoned while the rate increases to one in two for Black trans or nonbinary people.

In prisons, bodies are confined and categorized by rigid notions of gender to serve various agendas including the organization of forced penal labor where imprisoned people earn between 20-30 cents per hour for what is essentially enslaved labor, which decreases costs and increases the wealth of a penal system literally built on enslavement (Schwartzapfel 2018). Carceral networks are invested in compulsory cisgender and heterosexual normativity, explains Elias Vitulli (2013) in *Queering the Carceral: Intersecting Queer/Trans Studies and Critical Prison Studies,* the prescription for which poses life-threatening risks to trans and nonbinary people who experience disproportionately high rates of incarceration. In men's prisons, for example, concentrated masculinity naturalizes violence toward people seen as feminine or queer whereas the expectation in female prisons is for inmates to be docile and any deviation or gender-nonconformity is seen as a contributing factor of their incarceration (Vitulli, 117).

State violence against trans and nonbinary people is a byproduct of compulsory cisgender and hete-rosexual normativity that the PIC both hinges upon and reproduces. Compulsory heterosexuality is the process by which society assumes hetero-sexuality as a natural state and enforces behaviors and relationships that affirm its legitimacy onto subjects while disappearing behaviors and relationships that are seen as deviant or unnatural. "Gender normativity understood as a series of cultural, political, legal and religious assumptions that attempt to divide our bodies into two categories (men/women), is both a product of and a producer of the PIC," writes Eric Stanley, editor of *Captive Genders: Trans Embodiment and the Prison Industrial Complex* (2015). "We must pay attention," they continue, "to the ways in which the PIC harms trans/gender-non-conforming people and also to how the PIC produces the gender binary and heteronormativity itself" (Stanley 12).

Stanley defines the "webs of surveillance" in society that touch queer people before they ever enter a jail or prison as modes of policing trans and nonbinary bodies that start from childhood at home, continue through the education system, and compound in adulthood at the workplace, on public streets, and homeless shelters (Stanley, 13) where LGBTQ youth account for 40 percent of all homeless minors (Durso & Gates 2012). Societal gender norms push trans and nonbinary people into informal economic labor such as selling drugs and sex work for which they are disproportionately targeted by police for classist infractions like soliciting, truancy, and loitering (Stanley, 13).

"When people are released, especially those with felonies, the issues that found them in the prison industrial complex are dramatically compounded," says Stanley, who hauntingly defines prisons as "spaces of suspended death" during an interview (Rasheed 2014) in which they argue that advocates of prison reform fail to acknowledge that the very process of reform expands the PIC through so-called progressive solutions that alter and spread state power rather than shrink it. "The distinction between reform and abolition is vital" because reform assumes that the system is broken (and can be fixed) whereas abolition serves as "a political commitment that makes the PIC impossible," Stanley explains. The debate on reform versus abolition within nonhuman animal advocacy runs along similar lines where more laws translate into more opportunities for the legal system to diminish the agency of human bodies. Industries that commodify nonhuman animals share with prisons in their production of wealth through the commodification of captivity.

Like prisons, farms are heavily gendered spaces. Animal agriculture is an industry rooted in the heterosexist ideology of animal husbandry which hinges upon the denial of nonhuman animals' agency over their own bodies, sexuality, repro-duction, and ability to experience pleasure. Though homosexuality is common among nonhuman animals just as it is among humans (Sommer 2006), farmed animals are denied both the ability to pursue behaviors that are natural to them and the agency to form relationships with mates of their choosing. "In animal agriculture—whether on factory farms or animal farms—everything depends on reproduction," writes Ecofeminist vegan scholar pattrice jones, who charts animal agriculture's enforcement and exploitation of heterosexuality through repetitive breeding, birthing, egg laying, and milking, "from the electro-ejaculation of bulls to the confinement of fragile 'broiler breeder' hens with heavyweight roosters made sex-mad by starvation, numerous cruel and unusual strategies ensure that no farmed animal opts out of compulsory heterosexuality (jones 2014).

There is specific protocol for nonhuman animals based on the profitability of their assigned gender: male chicks are macerated hours after hatching because they cannot lay eggs or grow large breasts and thighs while female chicks are raised to become broiler hens for their flesh or laying hens for their eggs. Male calves are killed as infants for veal or they live a year or two longer to be killed for other cuts of beef while females are used for their milk. (After their lactation ceases, they, too, are sold for their flesh and ground into hamburger.) In *The*

*Sexual Politics of Meat* (1990)*,* Carol J. Adams distinguishes between the animalized and feminized proteins to unpack the gendered and sexual politics of nonhuman animal consumption. "Through the animalizing of protein animals are reduced to being a means to our ends, converted from being some*one* to some*thing*. They are seen as bodies to be manipulated as incubators of protein," Adams writes (emphasis hers). "A corollary and prelude to animalized protein is feminized protein: milk and eggs" she continues. In both instances, nonhuman animals are treated as objects not living beings, but in terms of feminized proteins, nonhuman animals are oppressed specifically for their ability to "produce food from their own body while living," she concludes (Adams, 52).

Nonhuman animals and farm workers aren't the only beings who are harmed by animal agriculture. As meat industries reap billions, they outsource the damages caused by industrialized practices to the environment, public health, and the economy, the burden of which is borne primarily by impoverished Communities of Color that reside near the farms where waste run-off, ground water contamination, soil erosion, and air pollution adversely affect their quality of life (Environmental Working Group 2016). These residents develop chronic illnesses, lose property value, and endure the constant stench of ammonia and fecal matter (Cooke 2016), which has prompted affected communities across the US to organize and file lawsuits against farms and the EPA for damages. But they face an uphill battle against wealthy, influential corporations that aggressively lobby their business interests to state and federal officials (Center for Biological Diversity 2019).

## Veganizing the Carceral State

The trend in animal advocacy is to also appeal to the power of the state on behalf of nonhuman animals, which poses grave setbacks in its appeal to the larger anti-oppression movement. "Among progressive social movements, the nonhuman animal rights movement stands as a notable exception to an overriding trend of advocacy against tough-on-crime policies," writes Justin Marceau (2019), law professor, former public defender and author of *Beyond Cages: Animal Law and Criminal Punishment.* According to Marceau (2019), it is paradoxical that a movement would pursue "radically progressive social reform through regressive social policies," displaying a willfully ignorant "fidelity to and support for a proven system of human oppression and suffering as an assumed vehicle for undermining the structural oppression of non-humans." Marceau (2019) charts how nonprofit organizations like the Animal Legal Defense Fund (ALDF) and the American Society for the Prevention of Cruelty to Animals (ASPCA) support the detainment and deportation of undocumented immigrants, the incarceration of minors, increased felony sentences, and animal cruelty offender registries.

Founded in 1866, the ASPCA passed one of the first pieces of anti-cruelty legislation in the U.S. which granted them power to conduct investigations and make arrests (Finsen, 1994). The ASPCA boasts an unprecedented alliance with the New York Police Department (NYPD) that funds special officers to recue animals, provide treatment and placement, and make arrests of which there were 131 in 2018 (ASPCA, 2014). The NYPD is the oldest, largest, and most militarized police force in the US (Ganeva & Gottendeiner, 2012) with a history of corruption, violence against queers, trans women, and sex workers, racial profiling of Black and Brown adults and youth, unlawful surveillance of Muslims, excessive force against peaceful protestors, and fatal shootings by police of unarmed Black people (Make the Road NY, 2012).

The ALDF works more directly with the courts and has privatized prosecution in states by subsidizing the costs of local law enforcement to investigate and prosecute nonhuman animal abuse cases. They support felony convictions and perpetuate moral panic that nonhuman animal abusers will inevitably become violent toward humans (ADLF 2018). Their tough-on-cruelty campaigns are byproducts of racist tough-on-crime policies passed down from the Johnson, Reagan, and Clinton administrations that took rights away from incarcerated people and incentivized state law enforcement to be more punitive (Robinson 2016). This approach upholds the belief that locking individuals behind bars will solve a complex social problem.

Locking a person behind bars does not address the circumstances or environmental factors that contribute to their violence against nonhuman animals. While their incarceration may temporarily prevent them from committing the same type of harm, it does not allow for transformation and healing of the individual, the community they belong to, and the being(s) who have been harmed. As I've explored earlier in this essay, because of systemic racial and gendered violence that disproportionately harm marginalized communities, the work of organizations like the ALDF and the ASPCA to enforce animal protection through the carceral state and thus amplify its reach, their work does and will continue to treat the symptoms (behavior) rather than systemic oppression, which will in turn contribute to more queer and BBIPoC being imprisoned by the PIC.

## Anti-Carceral Queer Veganism

The narratives of modern mainstream vegan and LGBTQ movements have become defined by their alignment with hegemonic power rather than their subversion of it. Reliance upon recognition from the state through animal rights-based legislation runs parallel to the LGBTQ movement that pivoted from starting riots in protest of the legal system to the demand for rights and protection under it.

"The heavy price of institutionalized protection is always a measure of dependence and agreement to abide by the protector's rules," writes political theorist Wendy Brown in her book *States of Injury: Power and Freedom in Late Modernity* (1995). It is the sharing of power, she explains, not the regulation of it, that leads to liberation. Once a movement begins to mobilize around emancipation, which are given by the state—rather than liberation, which is taken by the people—the collective power of the group is exchanged for the assigned rights of individuals who must become coherent legal subjects in order to gain status through their assimilation into the state. But though the mainstream version of a movement is its most visible arm, it by no means outweighs the masses of people striving for radical political change through collective power.

We cannot attempt to solve one thread of an interconnected web of oppressions while denying the others exist. This applies to vegans and nonvegans, queers and heterosexuals, and prison abolitionists and reformers alike. In *Striving with Systems,* Black queer vegan scholar Christopher Sebastian McJetters calls for a liberatory, rather than emancipatory, anticapitalist radical vegan philosophy that avoids the pitfalls of the kind of reformist thought that has held movements back in the past because "the system only finds new ways of enslaving us" (2017).

At the core of oppressive carceral institutions in the U.S. that exploit humans and nonhuman animals is the system of capitalist white supremacy and its deconstruction is central to any movement that seeks to return power to the people. To overlook or actively ignore the role of speciesism in the construction of white supremacy, colonialism, and extractive capitalist expansion (which are at the heart of heteropatriarchal carceral system) allows the central argument for racial hierarchies to continue unchallenged. "It was whiteness that politicized 'human' as an identity separate from and superior to 'animal,' a shift that allowed for the enslavement of black people because we were (and are) dehumanized, nee [sic] de-personified, in the eyes of whiteness," McJetters continues.

When it comes to nonhuman animals, we can no longer hide or disappear their lives from society or from our collective conscience. "Animal exploitation is the bedrock of imperialist white supremacist capitalist cis-heteropatriarchy," McJetters concludes. "You want to abolish oppression, you gotta include other species." To hold nonhuman animals at a distance in our minds as philosophical quandaries to ponder or to infantilize them as dependent beings without agency is to ignore the reality of their circumstances. They are living autonomous beings who have complex and emotional inner lives, who exhibit the full spectrum of sexuality and gender, who cultivate their own language and culture, who choose mates and companions and create families, who seek shelter, nourishment, and happiness, and who are incarcerated by the billions as political prisoners in zoos, circuses, research laboratories, farms, and slaugh-

terhouses from which they actively seek to escape
(Pittman 2017).

We cannot decry the prison industrial complex
and justify the factory farm when they are different
parts of the same carceral network. If we are to
imagine a world where prisons cease to exist, we
must include the complex systems of captivity that
imprison nonhuman animals, too, recognizing that
solidarity does not stop at one's species. "The true
potential of queer and trans politics cannot be
found in attempting to reinforce out tenuous right
to exist by undermining someone else's," Stanley
explains. "If it is not clear already, we are all in this
together. To claim our legacy of beautiful possibility
is to begin practicing ways of being with one
another and making movement that sustain all life
on this planet, without exception" (Stanley, 43).

*Cited Works*

Borlik, J. (2012). Butterball Worker Pleads Guilty to
Felony Cruelty to Animals. *Fox 8 Cleveland*.

Brown, W. (1995). *States of Injury: Power and
Freedom in Late Modernity*. Princeton University
Press.

Cooke, C. (2016). North Carolina's Factory Farms Produce 15,000 Olympic Pools Worth of Waste Each Year. *Civil Eats.*

Davis, A. (2016). *Freedom Is a Constant Struggle: Ferguson, Palestine, and the Foundations of a Movement.* Haymarket.

Davis, A. (1998). Masked Racism: Reflections on the Prison Industrial Complex. *Race Forward.*

DelReal, J. A. (2016). Several members of Trump's agriculture committee have supported legal status for undocumented workers. *The Washington Post.*

Dolovich, S. (2011). Exclusion and Control in the Carceral State. *Berkeley Journal of Criminal Law*, 16 (2).

Dumont, D. M., et al. (2012). Public health and the epidemic of incarceration. *Annual Review of Public Health*, 33: 325-39.

Durso, L. and Gates, G. J. (2012). Serving Our Youth: Findings from a National Survey of Service Providers Working with Lesbian, Gay, Bisexual, and Transgender Youth who are Homeless or At Risk of Becoming Homeless. *The Williams Institute with True Colors Fund and The Palette Fund.*

Ganeva, T. and Gottendeiner, L. (2012). Nine terrifying facts about America's biggest police force. *Salon*.

Hinton, E. (2016). *From the War on Poverty to the War on Crime: The Making of Mass Incarceration in America*. Harvard University Press.

jones, p. (2014). Eros and the Mechanisms of Eco-Defense *in* Carol J. Adams and Lori Gruen (eds), *Ecofeminism: Feminist Intersections with Other Animals & the Earth*. Bloomsbury Academic: 91-106.

Kaeble, D. and Cowhig, M. (2018). Correctional Populations in the United States, 2016. *US DoJ Bureau of Justice Statistics*

Katzenstein, M. F. and Waller, M.R. (2015). Taxing the Poor: Incarceration, Poverty Governance, and the Seizure of Family Resources." *Perspectives on Politics*, 13(3):638-656.

Kirts, L. (2018). Coming Out as Vegan: The Cultural Overlap of Being Vegan and Queer. *Jarry Magazine*, 6: 58-65.

Kirts, L. (2019). The Exploitation of Factory Farms Doesn't Stop at Animals. *Tenderly*.

Marceau, J. (2019). Social Change, Animal Rights, and Incarceration. Cambridge University Press.

Marceau, J. (2019). *Beyond Cages: Animal Law and Criminal Punishment*. Cambridge University Press.

McJetters, C. S. (2017). Exploring Radical Veganism. *Striving with Systems*.

McLeod, S. (2018). The Stanford Prison Experiment. *Simply Psychology*.

Meyer, I., Flores, H., A. R., Stemple, L., Romero. A.P., Wilson, B. D. M., and Herman, J.L. (2017). Incarceration Rates and Traits of Sexual Minorities in the United States: National Inmate Survey, 2011–2012. *American Journal of Public Health*, 107: 267-273.

Morin, K. (2018). *Carceral Space, Prisoners and Animals*. Routledge.

Muller-Harris, D. L. (2001). Animal Violence Court: A Therapeutic Jurisprudence-Based Problem-Solving Court for the Adjudication of Animal Cruelty Cases Involving Juvenile Offenders and Animal Hoarders. *Animal Law Review*, 17(2):313-336.

Pachirat, T. (2013). *Every Twelve Seconds: Industrialized Slaughter and the Politics of Sight*. Yale University Press.

Petersen, M. B. et al. (2012). To punish or repair? Evolutionary psychology and lay intuitions about modern criminal justice. *Evolution and Human Behavior*, 33(6): 682-695.

Potter, G. (2013). The History of Policing in the United States. *Prison Policy Initiative*.

Rasheed, K. J. (2014). The Carceral State. *The New Inquiry*.

Rep. Deutch, Theodore E. (2019). H.R.724 - Preventing Animal Cruelty and Torture Act. *116th Congress*.

Riess, R., Jackson, A., and Lou, M. (2019). An arrest has been made in the Fair Oaks Farms animal cruelty case. *CNN*.

Ritchie, A. J. and Jones-Brown, D. (2017). Policing Race, Gender, and Sex: A Review of Law Enforcement Policies. *Women & Criminal Justice*, 27(1): 21-50.

Robinson, N. J. (2016). Kool-Aid and Cyanide. *Jacobin*.

Runkle, N. (2012). Making History: Butterball Case Marks First-Ever Felony Conviction for Cruelty to Factory-Farmed Birds. *Mercy for Animals*.

Ryan, H. (2019). The Queer History of the Women's House of Detention. *The Activist History Review*.

Sawyer, W. and Wagner, P. (2019). Mass Incarceration: The Whole Pie 2019. *The Prison Policy Initiative*.

Schwartzapfel, B. (2018). Taking Freedom: Modern-day Slavery in America's Prison Workforce. *Pacific Standard*.

Sokol, J. (2016). Women on the line: A review of workplace gender issues in the US poultry industry. *Oxfam America*.

Solotaroff, P. (2013). Animal Cruelty is the Price We Pay for Cheap Meat. *Rolling Stone*.

Sommer, V. and Vasey, P.L. (2006). *Homosexual Behaviour in Animals: An Evolutionary Perspective*. Cambridge University Press.

Springate, M. E. (2016). Ed. LGBTQ America: A Theme Study of Lesbian, Gay, Bisexual, Transgender, and Queer History. *National Park Foundation*.

Stanley, E. A. (2015). Ed. *Captive Genders: Trans Embodiment and the Prison Industrial Complex*. AK Press.

Stuesse, A. (2016). *Scratching Out a Living: Latinos, Race, and Work in the Deep South*. University of California Press.

*US Department of Labor* (2013). Highest Incidence Rates of Total Nonfatal Occupational Illness Cases, Table SNR12. *Bureau of Labor Statistics*.

Vitulli, E. W. (2013). Queering the Carceral: Intersecting Queer/Trans Studies and Critical Prison Studies. *GLQ: A Journal of Lesbian and Gay Studies*, 19(1): 111-123.

Wagner, P. and Rabuy, B. (2017). Following the Money of Mass incarceration. *Prison Policy Initiative*.

FELIZ BRUECK AND McNEILL

## *Beyond Binaries: An Interspecies Case for They/Them Pronouns*

Patti Nyman

As a queer and nonbinary person, as well as a participant in the animal rights and vegan movements over the past 5 years, I've observed ways in which these movements could potentially be strengthened by learning from gender justice work. Specifically, the interaction between my nonbinary identity and the social worlds in which I find myself has revealed to me that there are few areas of human interaction that don't invoke the gender binary. Whether we're referring to humans or nonhumans, babies or adults, or objects like cars or boats, communicating in today's white supremacist capitalist cishetero patriarchy involves a constant barrage of he's and she's.

This linguistic gendering most often serves one of two purposes. It can function to personify and identify individuals, like when we ask, "Who is she?" It can also function to signal ownership and subjugation through the exclusive use of "female" pronouns like when people say, "I just bought this boat, isn't she beautiful?" In this sense, whether conscious or not, linguistic gendering serves to reinforce dominant social structures of oppression and makes identifying a being or thing as "she" or "he" a precursor to being known and valued.

The narrative that places the white, cisgender, heterosexual, able-bodied human man at the top of the social hierarchy supports itself through the continual reinstatement of the "it-ness" of perceived others. In everyday language, this commonly presents itself when folks refer to nonhuman animals as "it" rather than with pronouns, and we also hear this when marginalized humans are intentionally demeaned. The "it-ness" of falling outside of "she" or "he" is perhaps most striking in the common question asked of pregnant people, "Is *it* a boy or a girl?" It is as though one must enter consciousness through "he" or "she" to be recognizable as human at all.

It's time to change this.

We need to avoid the default of going through the binary to get to personhood, to avoid requiring gender categorization at all in order to be morally recognizable. Unfortunately, what we find in many circles of animal advocates is that the move toward recognizing the personhood of nonhumans only goes so far as to adopt a "he or she" approach to pronouns for animals. This excludes trans, nonbinary, and non-Eurocentric linguistic possibilities entirely and misses an important opportunity to address animal liberation and gender justice at the same time.

How we communicate reflects how we think, and how we think is reflected in the society we work to create. As we move toward recognizing the personhood and moral standing of nonhumans through rescue and sanctuary, telling their stories, and talking about their relationships, we can also take a more consistently anti-oppressive stance by moving toward using "they" and "them" much of the time. Unless we are drawing attention to the particular plight of females or males within particular industries, the liberating linguistic step after "it" is "them."

FELIZ BRUECK AND McNEILL

## *Queer Vegan Politics and Consistent Anti-Oppression*

*Shiri Eisner*

My name is Shiri, and as I write these words, I am 37 years old and live in Tel Aviv, Israel/Occupied Palestine. I have been an activist on various social justice and radical left issues for the past 15 years. As a person whose identities straddle a number of intersections, my politics are and always have been deeply affected by my life, experiences, and identities.

I'm bisexual and genderqueer. I started identifying as bi when I was 13 and joined the Tel Aviv gay and lesbian community (as it was called back then – bi, trans, and ace erasure included) when I was in high school in the mid-90s. I attended Tel Aviv's first gay youth group and marched in its first Pride Parade without ever knowing they were the first. I started my radical queer activism in 2005, my bisexual activism in 2008, and published a book about bisexual politics, *Bi: Notes for a Bisexual Revolution*, in 2013.

I'm also a feminist, this being one of my oldest political identities. I started my feminist activism in

2005 around the time when I started my BA in gender studies. Living in a patriarchal world where misogyny is so deeply embedded and all-consuming, feminism has given me the language and tools to name and resist women's oppression. In particular, intersectional feminism, queer feminism, and anarcha-feminism serve as immense sources of inspiration and empowerment as guides on how to practice justice that leaves no one outside and can transform reality.

I'm Mizrahi (Arabic Jewish) and also mixed-race. Being visibly Brown, my life has been laced with experiences of both covert and overt racism although I couldn't name these experiences as such until I came into the Mizrahi movement around 2010. The zionist myth that "we are all Jewish here" and that "racism is a thing of the past" runs deep in our culture. Outside of Israel, on the other hand, people often falsely assume that all Jews are Ashkenazi (European), that they enjoy unconditional white privilege, and that Jewish People of Color don't exist. Since joining the Mizrahi movement, I learned much about recognizing, identifying, and naming our oppression as well as the many ways it echoes and connects with that of Black, Indigenous, and other People of Color.

I'm also an anarchist and anti-zionist and have been since high school. Zionist culture is deeply embedded with racism, militarism, and colonialism that carry over to every nook and cranny in our lives, every sphere, and every issue. Nothing is separate from the occupation, apartheid, and ethnic cleansing against the Palestinians. Every single aspect of our lives – from the smallest to the greatest – is controlled and constructed by it, built upon it, and unavoidable in its constant, mundane, unbearable cruelty. I feel that in many ways, it is impossible to truly support justice in Israel/ Occupied Palestine without also opposing and resisting the horrors perpetrated against the Palestinians. For this reason, I have been involved in Palestine solidarity and pro-BDS[19] work for many years now through writing, organizing, and protests.

I'm disabled/chronically ill, having been living with fibromyalgia for nearly 10 years now. As I started engaging with disability politics, I discovered an amazing richness and depth of knowledge and understanding. Disability discourses hold so much knowledge about sustainability, ethics, survival, and resistance that it nearly takes my breath away. In addition, since almost all oppressive systems (capitalism, patriarchy, and whiteness to name just a

---

[19]Boycott, Divestment, and Sanctions against apartheid Israel.

few) so clearly coalesce around disability, some of the most incisive analyses that I have seen have come from the disability justice movement. Becoming connected with this movement has also led me to one of the most beautiful and wisest community I've ever known – that of queer disabled People of Color, whose brilliance and insights never cease to amaze me.

All of these identities and experiences, as well as many others, have led me to a political stance that embraces all oppressed people and aspires to resist all dominant power wherever it may be – on every axis and at every intersection, never using one to perpetuate the other, or throwing anyone under the bus. I will refer to this concept within this text as *multidimensional anti-oppression* politics or activism). All of these things also serve as the basis for my understanding of all types of oppression as inextricably connected and of leftist and social justice activist work as part of a broad and all-encompassing effort to dismantle all oppression. I will refer to this concept within this text as *consistent anti-oppression* politics or activism, a term coined by activist-author Julia Feliz Brueck.

I've been vegan for 16 years now and consider veganism an enormous part of my political philosophy. The following text comes from my experiences in the movements I took part in throughout the years. In it, I invite other people and communities to have a look at how social justice work can look when it incorporates nonhuman animal liberation.

## Israel/Occupied Palestine

Writing about Israel/Occupied Palestine often requires navigating problematic outside perceptions about this place, culture, and the people living here. Colonial zionist perceptions of Israel view it as a beacon of advancement and culture within a "hostile" and "backward" Brown environment. Others, no less colonial, view it as part of its "backward" surroundings, a place that is itself "wild" and "uncultured," where Brown "savages" wage endless irrational wars against one another. The logic of white saviorism says that what the people of this area need is the "care" and "guidance" of the West's "higher" moral values – a problem also evident in the amounts of white North American or European activists who travel here to volunteer while believing they have the solution to our problems.

Another problematic stance present in many discourses around zionist Israel is antisemitism. This view considers Jewish people as inherently and consistently oppressive. Specifically, in left and social justice discourses, zionist Jews are often dehumanized or presented through antisemitic tropes. Israeli politics are often oversimplified in ways that erase the complexity of Israel's particular case of settler colonialism. Jewish people in these leftist and social justice communities are often questioned on their position regarding this issue, even in completely unrelated contexts. Often, they also encounter demands to explain and apologize for Israel's actions. On the other hand, some people naively justify and defend zionist Israelis often using a "not all Israelis"-type argument (similar to the infamous "not all men"), by which they mean that not all Jewish Israelis are complicit in the occupation, apartheid, and ethnic cleansing against the Palestinians. Many people seem unaware of the overwhelming levels of fascism, racism, and militarism in Jewish Israeli culture and of the fact that all Jewish Israelis benefit from these horrors regardless of their personal opinions. Because of this, they interpret problematic acts and statements in highly charitable ways, while playing down the general context. They tend to absolve single-issue Israeli social justice movements of their complicity in this toxic system, not acknowledging that all civil society in Israel is founded on it.

All of these strands make it difficult to speak about Israel/Occupied Palestine in a way that acknowledges and holds space for its complexity. In this context, positive statements might be taken as a sign that Israel truly is the "enlightened" "western" beacon that it claims to be; alternatively, it may make one suspected of supporting zionism. Negative statements, on the other hand, may feed into antisemitic or orientalist perceptions about Israel/Occupied Palestine and the Middle East as inherently oppressive or "backward."

This is all the more complicated as zionist propaganda appropriates human rights and nonhuman animal rights discourses. In recent years, this type of propaganda has focused its attention on two main issues: LGBT rights, through what we call *pinkwashing*, and veganism, through what we call *veganwashing*. The first tries to paint Israel as "the gay Mecca" of the Middle East while the second tries to present it as one of the most vegan-friendly countries in the world. This is done as a rhetorical tactic in order to market Israel as the "progressive," "liberal" haven of the Middle East – in attempt to draw attention away from Israel's many war crimes and human rights violations.

Most efforts to resist this tactic have been made as part of (and in solidarity with) the Boycott,

Divestment, and Sanctions (BDS) movement, which focuses on working against this propaganda and refocusing the discussion on where it's relevant. The BDS is a global movement for a comprehensive economic, cultural, and academic boycott of zionist Israel. It lists three goals: ending the occupation and colonization of all Arab lands and dismantling the Separation Wall; full equality for Arab-Palestinian citizens of Israel; and acknowledging the rights of Palestinian refugees to return to their homes. The BDS focuses not only on ending Palestinians' oppression, but also in building a better society; thus, the BDS endorses and is endorsed by many queer, feminist, vegan, and other social justice organizations. I encourage my readers to learn more about this movement and to support it however they can.

Amidst all of this complexity, this text is not intended as a story about a strange and faraway land. Neither is it meant as an exoticized account of a "developing" movement in a "backward" part of the world. The references I make to problematic aspects in local politics do not constitute appeals to a higher, whiter morality, nor do they insinuate an inherent oppressiveness within the people of this place. Likewise, describing the better parts of our politics and movements is not intended as support of zionist pinkwashing and veganwashing propaganda depicting Israel as inherently more "liberal," "tolerant," or "progressive" than its surrounding cultures.

What I do mean is to use the example of Israeli social justice and leftist communities to show how veganism can be consistent with these politics and with all intersecting struggles. Far from being considered as separate from these movements, or as being in conflict with them, much of our communities here practice *consistent anti-oppression veganism*. We do so by incorporating veganism and nonhuman animal liberation into our multidimensional work against oppression.

## White-Centered Veganism and Animal Rights

I am aware of the unfortunate fact that in North America and Europe, mainstream white-centered vegan/Animal Rights movements are often far from acknowledging intersecting oppression or incorporating it into their work. They often hijack conversations about human oppression to speak exclusively about nonhuman animals. Some phrase their messages through misogyny, racism, classism, ableism, and heteronormativity while others participate in dialogues and practices that throw other oppressed people under the bus. This

237

patronizing and marginalizing behavior has caused many leftist and social justice activists in these cultures to feel alienated from the concept of nonhuman animal rights and the practice of veganism and to perceive it as opposite to *multidimensional anti-oppression* work.

The Israeli nonhuman animal rights movement is certainly not free of these toxic approaches – in fact, they've only been increasing in recent years (as I will describe later in more detail). However, the movement here does have deep roots in intersecting leftist and social justice politics. For many years, much of the nonhuman animal liberation movement was engaged in consistent anti-oppression veganism – and much of our intersecting anti-oppression movements incorporated veganism (and still do).

Therefore, with the hope of illustrating the multiple ways in which veganism is compatible with consistent anti-oppression work and the ways in which they connect with each other, the following section begins through the telling of my experiences in various movements and continues with examples of how the local queer, bi, and trans communities have intersected with the struggle for animal rights. Lastly, I explain some of our understandings of the links between multidimensional oppression and veganism, which underlie the type of activism practiced by these communities.

## Leftists and Vegans and Queers, Oh My!

I was vegetarian for four years before I became vegan in 2004 at 21 years old. My vegetarianism started out as an "experiment." I used to love meat in all its forms – it was one of my favorite foods. I used to be one of those people who knew about veganism but completely rejected it. Two of my classmates in high school were vegan, and every now and again, one of them would reproach my meat eating. She used to say, "That's dead," and I would respond that I didn't care because it was tasty. I didn't give it any thought; it was such an ingrained, normalized part of my life.

Then, my boyfriend at the time became vegetarian. I don't remember us talking about it, but we must have. A few months after he started his vegetarian journey, I started out experimenting with vegetarianism; I stopped eating all forms of meat, telling myself it was a way of "testing my willpower." Thinking about it now, it seems obvious to me that I didn't choose this particular "test" for no reason. There were many other things that I loved, so why pick this? I now realize that I needed to stop eating meat so I could give space to my true thoughts and feelings about it: I have always loved all animals, have always felt connected to them, and always felt care and compassion for them. I needed to give space to those feelings outside of the context of eating meat in order to acknowledge that I didn't want to eat nonhuman animals. I didn't want to partake in the death and torture of living beings for whom I cared so deeply.

I remember the last time I ate meat knowingly: a few months after starting our vegetarianism, my boyfriend and I went to a restaurant to celebrate his 19th birthday. We decided to make an exception and allow ourselves to eat meat on that particular special occasion, but as we ate our meal, my heart began breaking. I couldn't stop thinking about the fact that we were eating the dead body of someone who used to be alive, whom I would have loved if I'd met. They were now lying dead – torn and dissected – on our plate being consumed by us. We were taking their death into our bodies. This realization was horrific. I felt a deep sense of grief. I could never eat meat again after that.

Looking back, I realized that my high school boyfriend and the friends that I had when I went vegan were also bisexual. More specifically, our culture was that of radical queer politics and multilayered anti-oppression politics in which we discussed the connections and intersections between different identities and different forms of oppression. Our veganism was no different, and we all thought about it as part of our underlying politics. In this way, my veganism also constitutes an inextricable part of my experience and identity as bisexual, as a feminist, and as a queer anarchist.

One year later, in 2005, I came into radical queer activism.[20] It felt like a breath of fresh air. I remember the huge sense of relief in finding out that there were other people (outside my small group of friends) who thought about politics the way I did. These were people who cared about *all the things* rather than just one or two, and they cared about how these things came together, including the echoes, the intersections, and the unity of struggles. This was pre-social media, no Facebook groups and no Tumblr. The internet was more dispersed, and to get to the really good things, you needed to know exactly what you were looking for and where to go. Activist communities were run mostly though mailing lists, and you needed to know they existed and who to talk to if you wanted

---

[20]As opposed to my early involvement with the mainstream "gay and lesbian" community in high school.

to join them. So finding out that there was a whole community centered around the same ideas was amazing to me.

The anarchist queer group Black Laundry started out from a Palestine solidarity action during the 2001 Tel Aviv Pride Parade. Participants took over the front of the parade, some of them topless, protesting the occupation, apartheid, and ethnic cleansing against the Palestinians, within the context of the Pride Parade and the LGBT community. This is the group that created the slogan "No pride in occupation," which survives to this day not just here but all over the world (including its variants, "No pride in war," "No pride in capitalism," etc.).[21] Afterwards, Black Laundry continued with activism that included a variety of issues, always drawing attention to their intersections and the interconnections between them. I remember seeing one of their fliers and how it beautifully weaved *all* of their stances together: queerness, anti-zionism, anti-militarism, anti-racism, anti-capitalism, feminism – *and* animal liberation. It felt like I had finally found my people. Unfortunately, however, their last year of activism was also 2005, the year I had found them.

---

[21]Specifically, this slogan is credited to Aeyal Gross, now a professor of law, and one of the key figures in queer theory in Israel/Occupied Palestine.

In the summer of 2006, the anarchist queer gathering, Queeruption, was held in Tel Aviv right as the second Lebanon war broke out. I was already regularly hanging out at the local infoshop, Salon Mazal,[22] which served as the social hub for this community (as well as others). The salon (as we used to call it) shared a space with the Veggie Bar, the best place to get a full vegan meal and a fruit shake for only 20 Shekels.[23] I joined the Queeruption's Pink-Black Bloc[24] in the demonstrations that were held against the war, and the more I went, the more I felt at home.

The Pink-Black Bloc only survived a few months, but for many of us, it had laid the groundwork for our activism to come.[25] This community was where

---

[22]Infoshop are community spaces where people can access anarchist literature and materials. Salon Mazal had a library, a store (selling books, zines, political T-shirts, and other things), and also served as a space for activist workshops, lectures, gatherings, and meetings.
[23]The equivalent of about $5 (USD).
[24]A black bloc is an anarchist group of protesters, usually as part of larger demonstrations. Traditionally, black bloc participants wear all black (the color of the anarchist flag). The pink-black bloc was a queer anarchist group, and concurrently, the participants wore pink and black clothes (the color of the queer anarchist flag).
[25]For much, much more about this, check out my article:

I'd met some of the people who pioneered the nonhuman animal rights movement in Israel/ Occupied Palestine in all their multidimensional anti-oppression glory, people like Yossi Wolfson, Yosef(a) Mekyton, Adi Winter, and others who are still active today and from whom I learned how deeply all our struggles are related to the oppression, and the liberation, of nonhuman animals. Simply put, nonhuman animal rights activism was prominently headed by anarchist queers and feminists. In fact, at that time, much of the vegan, radical queer, and intersectional feminist communities consisted of the same people.

Yossi and Yosef(a) ran a drag show at the time called "The Leah Goldberg and the Doe Mice Horror Show,"[26] described as "a political drag performance about animal and other rights" and "animal drag that curls the boundaries of feminist queer subversiveness, and gnaws at corporations. The doe mice take on and off various roles and unite all oppressed classes into a colorful extravaganza of resistance." Yossi and Yosef(a) performed as a cow

"Love, Rage and the Occupation: Bisexual Politics in Israel/Palestine."

[26]This is in reference to classical Israeli children's book "Room for Rent," by author Leah Goldberg. The book tells the story of a building housed with animals and their attempts to find a new neighbor to replace former tenant Sir Reginald Mouse. The show used it as a loose narrative basis.

and a chicken as the anchors of the show, while changing characters, multimedia formats (theater, musical performance, video, and more), and touching on a variety of intersecting and radical political issues. By doing animal drag, the Doe Mice sought to draw attention to the arbitrariness of socially constructed differences between human and nonhuman animals and to deconstruct the oppressive hierarchical binary of human vs. animal. Using this premise to address multiple types of oppression, they formed a coherent political language that was grounded in the intersection of queerness (drag) and veganism (animality).

In 2008, I began my bisexual activism establishing *Panorama – Bi and Pansexual Feminist Community*. This was the second bi organization to exist in Israel/Occupied Palestine (after our predecessors, *Bisexuals in Israel*, had stopped their activity), and there was little to no bi community as such as at the time. This was around the time when the radical queer community started its offshoots as what would become the trans community and the bi community (with huge overlaps between all of them, of course). Panorama was part of this trend. Since there was no established bi community, I started our organization together with activists I knew through the radical/multidimensional queer/feminist/vegan community. And so, of course, in addition to everything else (anarchism, anti-zionism, feminism, etc.), Panorama was also always vegan. Meaning that just like the animal rights movement at the time was largely headed by queers and feminists, those emerging bi, trans, and queer communities were largely headed by vegans. Specifically, for the bi community here, veganism and nonhuman animal liberation were at the core of its inception.

In 2010, Yosef(a), Tal(y) Wozner, and Eilam Bar Shalom started Karbolet, ("chicken comb" in Hebrew), the first chicken sanctuary in Israel/Occupied Palestine for survivors of the factory farming industry. The house where they lived, with a yard for the chickens, not only served as a sanctuary but also as a center for our various communities. All the people who lived there were radical queers who engaged in multidimensional anti-oppression work, members of the budding bi and trans communities as well as all the other movements already mentioned above. The house and everything it stood for was built on the intersection and lives of queer vegans.

In 2012, Panorama organized the *Festibi* – the first bi+ conference in Israel/Occupied Palestine.[27]

---

[27]The organizers were: Alon Zivony, Alona Sherf, Dana Peleg, Daniel (DanVeg) Sigawi (RIP), Purple ilth, Lilach Ben David,

We described it as "a non-profit communal, activist, and academic bisexual and pansexual conference, organized by bisexuals for the creation and empowerment of our community" (Lorde 2007). This was a radical and social justice-focused conference that included panels, lectures, and workshops around issues like bisexual boundary transgression, bi activist history, intersections of bi and trans, bisexuality in geek culture, radical bi politics, safer sex, DIY, and more.

While planning the conference, we put a lot of thought and work into making the space as accessible as possible. Participation was completely free of charge, the conference was held in a wheelchair (and otherwise) accessible venue, we had a sexual safety team to handle cases of harassment and to make sure everyone was comfortable, and we had volunteers transcribe every lecture and panel for the benefit of deaf and hard of hearing people.

One of the most complex and greatest logistic successes we had was no doubt the food. During the conference, we served three full vegan meals, and they were free for anyone who wanted to eat with us. The kitchen (operated by volunteers) was run by

Shirley-Justin Roitman, Tal(y) Wozner, Yoni Duck, and me.

Lilach Ben David, who was one of most prominent nonhuman animal rights activists in Israel/Occupied Palestine, and one of the leaders of the bi and trans communities. Each meal included multiple options and was served using biodegradable disposable tableware. We did all of this with a budget of around ILS 700,[28] most of which was spent on the food. The same plan was repeated in the following *Festibi+* conference held in 2015.[29] To this day, these two events set a shining example on how to make spaces truly and deeply accessible and how to integrate veganism along with other intersecting social justice politics and practice.

## Consistent Anti-Oppression Veganism

However, consistent anti-oppression veganism in Israel/Occupied Palestine doesn't just only rely on integration through practice. It also relies on a strong political framework, which weaves together intersecting political understandings of both human and nonhuman oppression.

---

[28] The equivalent of about $200 (USD).

[29] The organizers were: Atalia Israeli-Nevo, Aviv Sela, Chen Keller, Daniel (DanVeg) Sigawi (RIP), Hilla ohen, Ira Kontorovky, Lilach Ben David, Pablo Utin, Purple Filth, Tal(y) Wozner, Tanya Rubinstein, and Shlomi Fogel.

We see various forms of oppression not as isolated but as integrated and supported by one another, all part of one coherent system intended to maintain dominant power. Our struggles for liberation are not contradictory of one another – they are complementary. Different axes of oppression are not only connected at their intersections but also reflect one another and coalesce – including in purportedly "different" contexts. We find similarities and connections between different axes of oppression both inside and outside of their intersections. To take an example, the connections between ableism and misogyny don't only exist in the experience of disabled women. Instead, ableism and misogyny have similarities as ideologies, and they sometimes affect people in similar ways. Along with other dominant ideologies, they are enforced by the same systems, perpetuate the same values, and all belong to a larger coherent whole that is hegemony. These connections exist between all types of oppression. Therefore, all types of oppression are inextricably interconnected.

This idea is expressed through the term "unity of struggles," an idea so complementary to the understanding of oppression as multidimensional that for many of us, these two represent the very same thing. Multidimensional anti-oppression politics recognize the overlap between various types of oppression as they pertain to individuals, or communities, located at the intersection of two or more marginalized categories. It recognizes that, as famously worded by Audre Lorde, "There is no such thing as a single-issue struggle because we do not live single-issue lives" (Lorde 2007). Concurrently, the idea of the unity of struggles recognizes this overlap as it pertains to different, only seemingly separate, categories. The overlaps that still exist even for people who are not positioned at the intersection but still experience these connections because of the similar ways that oppression works.

And so, side by side with feminism, anti-racism, bi, trans and queer liberation, disability justice, anti-capitalism, and anti-zionism, our communities also speak about nonhuman animal liberation. We count it among the axes of oppression that we struggle against. English-speaking social justice communities dedicated to multidimensional anti-oppression work understand that single issue struggles are incomplete if they don't also include the people at the intersections. For example, feminism is considered incomplete if it doesn't also include bi, trans, nonbinary, and queer women, Black women, Indigenous women, and all other Women of Color as well as working-class women, sex workers, or disabled women. Similarly, in our communities, struggles against oppression are considered incomplete if they don't also include nonhuman animal liberation. We acknowledge the ways in which speciesism[30] and the oppression of non-human animals are interlinked with other types of oppression and the ways they echo and uphold each other. We speak about them in tandem and draw on their similarities to incorporate those understandings into the discourse that we create as well as in the activism that we do.

As opposed to single-issue white veganism, we don't employ these connections as a rhetorical device to hijack social justice issues. We don't use the oppression of marginalized humans as an empty tool for debate against nonvegans, without giving a second thought to the groups on whose backs those arguments are made. Instead, we are deeply committed to all sides of this discussion, and actively work to end everyone's oppression – human and nonhuman animals.

When it comes to feminism, we speak about the ways in which misogyny and speciesism echo and enable each other: how women and other people of marginalized genders (MaGe, as coined by

---

[30]Speciesism is the dominant ideology according to which nonhuman animals are inferior to humans.

activist Crystal Michelle) are compared to other animals and as such viewed as inferior. The way images of human and nonhuman female-assigned bodies as objects of consumption bleed into each other: sexualized nonhuman animals on commercial ads inviting us to eat their flesh, pornographic images presenting people with breasts as milking cows, or images of these same bodies mapped by "meat sections;" the way the meat, dairy, and egg industries are founded and sustained on the exploitation of nonhuman animals' female-assigned anatomy. We speak about the construction of meat consumption as masculine and how murderous violence towards both female-assigned bodies and nonhuman animals is coded as inherent and mandatory to (toxic) masculinity (Jones 2005, Goldilocks 2012, Hertzanu 2014, Adams 2015). We acknowledge all the ways in which the oppression of women and other MaGe and the oppression of nonhuman animals uphold and reflect each other as well as the fact that a truly radical struggle (seeking comprehensive rather than cosmetic change) includes liberation for all of us.

In terms of antisemitism, we remember how the Nazis have used methods from the meat industry and slaughterhouses in their attempt to exterminate Jews and others, the way their racial eugenics was inspired by selective animal breeding.

We remember the way Nazis compared Jews to vermin and pigs and how they used this comparison to legitimize their crimes. We remember holocaust survivor Isaac Bashevis Singer, who wrote that "for the animals, it is an eternal Treblinka," as well as other holocaust survivors and former Nazi officers who have made the same comparison. And we are aware that many of the practices used by the Nazis against their victims are to this day routinely used by humans against nonhuman animals. We do this as Jews, many of whom have lost ancestors to the Holocaust and have grandparents who are Holocaust survivors. We refuse to distance ourselves from the distinction between humans and animals that was used to justify the Holocaust and the slaughter of human beings. The distinction that says some of us are inherently worthy of life while others are worthy of death (Patterson 2002).[31]

In terms of anti-racism, we acknowledge the way Black, Indigenous, and other People of Color have been, and still are, imagined as closer to nonhuman animals, and thus, less human than white people. This is evident through things like the

---

[31]This is not intended as condonement of non-Jews using this type of language and imagery. If you are not Jewish, unless you have expert knowledge and political awareness of both the Holocaust and animal oppression, this may carry problematic overtones and is best avoided.

human evolution "march of progress" illustrations in which each evolutionary step away from the ape becomes more Eurocentric in appearance. We also see "white man's burden" perceptions of Black, Indigenous, and other People of Color as closer to nature and therefore, "uncultured," "wild," "violent," "uncontrollable," or otherwise as "naïve" and in need of white "guidance." We see Indigenous people displaced in the Amazon and their homes ruined to clear more and more areas for the meat industry. We remember historical "human zoos," where Black, Indigenous, and other People of Color were exhibited side by side with nonhuman animals; we remember Black people enslaved, held, and worked as chattel by white colonizers and kidnappers; and we remember the literal white consumption of Black bodies (Ko 2019). We acknowledge the ways in which this oppression is justified through this link to nonhuman animals and resist the systems that uphold both.

As Mizrahis (Arabic Jews) in Israel/Occupied Palestine, we note how often we are described by Ashkenazis (European Jews) as "apes who just now climbed down from the trees," "wild beasts," or "black animals." We recognize that our image has been tied in with nonhuman animals and used to justify our oppression. We know that before white colonization of the Middle East and North Africa, our traditional diets were far less reliant on animal source foods (Wolfson 2017), that many of our foods still are, and acknowledge that many of us have found it easier to transition into veganism based on the knowledge of our traditional foods. We refuse to dissociate ourselves from other animals and to throw them under the bus. We refuse to "redeem" ourselves by claiming we do not deserve oppression because we are unlike them.

As bi, trans, and queer people, we note the way bisexuality is often tied to "primitive" stages of development and "lower" life forms and how bi people are considered as "wild," as having "uncontrollable urges," or as being "predatory." We acknowledge the way meat consumption is constructed not only as male but also as cishet while veganism and soy consumption is imagined as leading to homosexuality and feminization (gender transgression) of the cis male body. We see cis men's penises described as "meat" ("man meat," "meat rod," "meat popsicle") while sex between women is described as "vegetarian" and thus as lacking "the real thing." Here in Israel/Occupied Palestine, we remember the LGBTQ-phobic "Beast Parade," held several times in the past decade, in which farmed animals were paraded in Jerusalem by right wing fascists as a "protest" against Pride. We then see the very same people denying the existence of sexual and gender diversity in nature, telling us that we're "unnatural" while at the same time comparing us to nonhuman animals.

When it comes to disability justice, we acknowledge how ableist eugenics (much like racist eugenics) is inspired by selective animal breeding. We see human torture, killing, and eating of animal bodies being justified in ableist terms – "they aren't as intelligent as humans," "they don't think/feel like us," or "they're not able to liberate themselves." That way, animals are disabled as an inherent part of the meat, eggs, and dairy industries, their bodies bred and selected to raise production and thereby profit, leaving them sick, unable to move, or to sustain a healthy life. We see disabled people compared to nonhuman animals: "Otis the Frog Boy, Mignon the Penguin Girl," "Jo-Jo the Dog Faced Boy," Darwin's "Missing Link," and, of course, the "Elephant Man" (Taylor 2017). To paraphrase disabled author and activist Sunaura Taylor, if our oppression is entangled, our liberation is as well.

With regards to Palestine solidarity politics, we note the use, abuse, traumatizing, and killing of dogs by the Israeli Defense Forces (IDF) and the police when attacking Palestinians to maintain Israeli apartheid and control. We note zionist vegans describing Palestinians as being inherently cruel to nonhuman animals as a justification for the atrocities perpetuated against them. We acknow-ledge the deaths and injuries of both humans and nonhuman animals in Gaza under Israeli attacks and slaughter. We see animals' dead bodies roasted en masse as an Independence Day tradition, celebrating zionism, militarism, and ethnic cleansing with the slaughter of animals. Yet, we see the vegan-washing undertaken by the IDF and Israel, attempting to wash out Israel's negative image, and instead present it as a progressive and tolerant vegan utopia. We acknowledge the similarities between this practice and that of pinkwashing – the use of our bi, trans, and queer communities within zionist propaganda to do the same. And we act in solidarity with Palestinian animal rights activists, who work to promote "justice for both people and animals as an interlinked challenge, which can, and should, be tackled in tandem" (Palestinian Animal League website).

These ideas are all mainstream in our left and social justice communities who are engaged in multidimensional anti-oppression work. They are part of our discourse and our practice.

## Single-Issue Veganism

Over the last decade, veganism has gained enormous traction in Israel/Occupied Palestine to the extent of being a national trend. The increasing popularization of veganism has led to many different changes compared to what was before, many positive and many less so.

On the positive side, vegan food, as well as information and resources, has become exponentially more accessible here. With vegan products, vegan restaurants, free training programs for beginners, and vegan certification for food, products, and businesses, veganism is far easier now than ever before. When I first became vegan, not many restaurants, sellers, or service providers even knew what veganism was. Today, not only does everyone know about it, but many restaurants have their own vegan menus, or at the very least, mark the vegan dishes on their existing ones. That said, for those living in Tel Aviv, there's not even a need any more to eat at non-vegan restaurants because so many vegan ones exist at every price level and for every palate. With veganism being constantly on the rise, it can be arguably said that, except for traditionally vegan societies, there has never been a time or place where veganism was easier or more accessible than currently in Israel/Occupied Palestine (and especially Tel Aviv).

However, simultaneously with the movement's expansion, we have seen vegan politics taking a disturbing turn into the mainstream. Mizrahi poet and scholar, Sami Shalom Chetrit, once said, "The radicals shake the tree, and the liberals pick the fruit." This statement is relevant to most every social justice movement – the movement is established by radicals, who take up problematic and "controversial" issues and work to resist them through radical, often grassroots activism without resources and without outside support. At a certain point, the movement catches, more and more people join it, and while it expands, its radical ideas are eroded in favor of liberal ones – seeking to gain access to power and to amend the system rather than deconstruct and resist it. With liberal ideas come the resources –volunteers, money, media coverage, and institutionalization. The more mainstream the idea becomes, the more its discourses become narrow and fail to challenge dominant power.

The same has happened within the Israeli vegan/Animal Rights movement. While the popularization of veganism has been absolutely amazing, the shift in politics has been deeply disheartening. Over the last decade, the movement shifted from expressing itself in terms of resistance to speaking in the language of hegemony.

Much of the movement is currently concerned with vegan consumerism, with the goal of increasing the selection of vegan products and production under capitalism. Capitalism is now considered as the path towards veganism rather than as a generator of oppression against nonhuman animals and humans. We see many constructions of veganism in tandem with zionism and the occupation, speaking about veganism in the IDF, praising the "heroism" of the dogs exploited, tortured, and killed in the IDF's service, supporting Independence Day celebrations while only condemning their carnist aspect while imagining Palestinians as inherently cruel to other animals to justify military aggression. We also see animal rights spoken through misogynist, essentialist, and heteronormative terms through claims such as "cows' milk belongs 'only to their babies'," "a mother is always a mother," or that "a mother should always be with her children" and therefore, speaking in terms of what's "natural" instead of what's just. We see animal rights activists and organizations supporting and praising fascists, racists, misogynists, and LGBT-phobes if they express support or even openness to veganism. These are just some examples.

While veganism in our left and social justice communities engaged in multidimensional anti-oppression work has never lost its place, the mainstream core of the vegan movement has moved away from consistent anti-oppression politics. And so while many continue with their beautiful consistent anti-oppression animal rights work, it's no longer directed mainly outside of the movement at the general public. We now dedicate increasingly more energy and resources into resisting oppressive ideologies within the movement itself.

If you asked me which option was better: a small but radical animal liberation movement, or a large but mainstream one, I wouldn't be able to choose. The expansion of the movement was and still is incredible and has actively saved many nonhuman animals' lives by reducing their torture, killing, and consumption. However, the price attached to this is still hard to accept. Moving away from politics that embrace consistent anti-oppression, the nonhuman animal rights movement is now all too happy to throw every other oppressed group under the bus of single-issue veganism. Despite this, animal liberation activists that practice consistent anti-oppression continue their work, holding all our communities accountable and never relenting on fighting against oppression in the face of single-issue politics. As white feminism doesn't cancel out intersectional feminism, as gay assimilationism doesn't cancel out bi, trans, and queer liberation, as single-issue disability rights doesn't cancel-out the disability justice movement, nor does single-issue veganism cancel out the fight for nonhuman animal liberation. We hold space for all of these complexities and maintain our struggle against oppression in all its ways and forms.

## To Conclude

Multi-dimensional social justice politics teach us to fight for everyone, to incorporate everyone within our circle of personhood, community, and care. Radical politics teach us to resist all hierarchies and to dismantle every system that is used to imprison, exploit, and annihilate.

Nonhuman animals should not be left outside of our movements. They are inseparable from us, worthy of life, and worthy of liberation. If I were to make one wish within this text, it's that all social justice communities reflect on veganism, nonhuman animal liberation movement, and the animals themselves and that they consider them as worthy of our empathy and our political attention. This while never letting go of our commitment to consistently resisting oppression and making sure that the way we talk about and practice nonhuman animal liberation remains liberatory for everyone.

Until every cage is empty.

*Cited Works*

Adams, C. J. (2015). *The Sexual Politics of Meat*. Bloomsbury Academic.

Eisner, S. (2012). "Love, Rage and the Occupation: Bisexual Politics in Israel/Palestine." *Journal of Bisexuality*, 12(1): 80-137.

Eisner, S. (2013). *Bi: Notes for a Bisexual Revolution*. Seal Press.

Feliz, J. (2018). An Intro to Consistent Anti-Oppression Veganism. *Medium*: https://tinyurl.com/skl87vb

Festibi+ (2020). Conference invitation and schedule: https://tinyurl.com/qpx6mp6

Goldberg, L. (2018). *Room for Rent*. Gefen Publishing House.

Goldilocks, E. [Lilach Ben David]. "Oness Ba'aley Hachaim, Schitat Hanasheem: Ben Feminism Leshichrur Ba'aley Chaim" [The Rape of Animals, the Slaughter of Women: Between Feminism and Animal Liberation]. *Revachim Lifney Chaim* [*Profits before Lives*], WordPress, 24 March 2012. [In Hebrew]: https://tinyurl.com/rq8dp8j. Accessed 6 March 2020.

Hertzanu, S. (2014). Lo Shfanfanot Vello Behemoth: Nasheem Tzoadot Lema'an Ba'aley Chaim [Neither Bunnies nor Cows: Women Marching for Animals]. *Sicha Mekomit* [*Local Call*]. [In Hebrew]: https://tinyurl.com/r7ademy

jones, p. (2005). Their Bodies, Our Selves: Moving Beyond Sexism and Speciesism. *Satya*.

Ko, A. (2019). *Racism as Zoological Witchcraft: A Guide to Getting Out.* Lantern Books.

Lorde, A. (2007). *Learning from the 60s*. in Audre Lorde, *Sister Outsider: Essays & Speeches*. Crossing Press: 138.

Palestinian Animal League (2019). *Work in Palestine.* PAL: https://pal.ps/en/about-us/work-in-palestine

Patterson, C. (2002). *Eternal Treblinka: Our Treatment of Animals and the Holocaust*. Lantern Books.

Taylor, S. (2017). *Beasts of Burden: Animal and Disability Liberation*. The New Press.

Wolfson, Y. (2009). Haochel Shel Haoyev – Nakba, Colonialism, Vemazon [The Enemy's Food – Nakba, Colonialism, and the Politics of Nutrition]. *Mahapecha Mehamartef* [*A Revolution from the Basement*]. Self-published zine. [In Hebrew]: https://tinyurl.com/t7yagjc

## *Is Your Memory Long Enough for the Road Ahead? The Problem with Inclusion*

LoriKim Alexander

Don't include me. Don't include us. We, Trans, Nonbinary, and Queer Black and Brown people have been here.

We've been here in *all* movement spaces and in all the creations of movement philosophies. Whether cis and straight people like it or not and whether they have been able to reconcile this with their idea of what our liberation movements should look like, or the history they've been mistold, we've been here.

We've been here even when the LGBTQIA+ movements remained centered and focused on white Trans and Queer people. We've been here fighting for nonhuman animal rights in the vegan movement. We've also been here fighting for Black liberation. So speaking about including Trans and Queer Black and Brown people in LGBTQIA+ movement spaces and in vegan spaces is an insulting joke. But let's step back a bit and look at our liberation movements in a more holistic way.

Movement work is the ways in which we push back and through the colonization of earth and its beings. The name itself means action and implies fluidity. Let us think of liberation movements, the movements that work against the oppression of marginalized bodies, as we think of biodiversity. Biodiversity is not the whole collection of beings on earth going about their daily business with no thought for any other species around them. What make the ecosystems which sustain us work are the symbiotic (mutually beneficial) relationships and networks of connections which run deep and are inextricably linked. These relationships are vital to the survival of the individuals within them. When we remove one tiny piece of this framework, we herald the collapse of systems. As each system breaks down, the entire earth begins to crumble. For instance, gopher tortoises are long-living burrowing reptiles found in the Southeastern United States. They can burrow down up to roughly 50 feet. They spend most of their lives in these burrows. Their burrows are key habitats for over 350 species. The gopher tortoise is currently on the endangered species list and threatened with extinction because of habitat loss. Many of the species of snakes, insects, frogs, and birds like the burrowing owl that also use gopher tortoise burrows are either threatened or critically endangered as well. Gopher tortoises are very territorial, so how is it that they can allow these animals into their spaces? These are mutually beneficial relationships as the animals find shelter and help protect the gopher tortoises, who are vegans as well by the way.

Thinking about spaces that claim to be focused on liberation, we see that none of the systems of oppression are disconnected; they all stem from the white supremacist capitalist patriarchy that is both the spawn of and impetus for colonialism (hooks 2004). So how is it that we expect that liberation will come without a clear and consistent centering of the most marginalized and affected by these systems across species? True anti-oppression work is abolition work. In our movements for Black lives, we have pledged to center the most marginalized Black people, but are we forgetting the Black people who have lost limbs and lives in the slaughter-houses, chicken farms, and other extensions of these state-sanctioned carceral systems? Within movements, we must contentiously and persistently think about the ways in which we, Black and Brown people, as a wholly marginalized, yet global majority contribute to the marginalization and subjugation of other beings and are also oppressed by this.

Queer liberation spaces, unless they are speci-fically created by People of Color, have historically faltered in centering Black, Indigenous, and other

People of Color, and have also never thought to expand their notion of what marginalized bodies means to include non-human animals. Not in any larger sense. If we include veganism, it is as a "dietary restriction" for the humans in these spaces, not as a point of praxis or a liberatory tool.

In vegan spaces, we often claim to center non-human species. However, centering animals means decentering ourselves without losing ourselves in that process. Yet, even in vegan spaces, we are routinely centering animals by anthropomorphizing them. This means we are using human models for the emotions, actions, and intentions of non-human animals. We do not know how to center them without first looking to ourselves as a model. That needs work. This work will mean detaching ourselves from our misconceptions that cloud our understanding. And, family, we are cloudy. We have been made so by hundreds of years of misconceptions that have seeped in so deep that routing them out feels like ripping out an organ. They were never ours though, fam.

So, when we work to center Trans and Queer Black, Indigenous, and other People of Color within the liberatory praxis of veganism, this cannot be done without the input of Trans and Queer Black, Indigenous, and other People of Color. In fact, it has to be done by Trans and Queer Black Indigenous and People of Color folks. The same is true for LGBTQIA+ movements and spaces.

Don't come to us and say you want to be inclusive, intersectional, and celebrate diversity if you don't come to us first before you create your spaces. Don't. Include. Me. Create the space with us in mind. You follow our lead. Hell, *unu* do this in everything else? In fashion, mannerisms, language, liberation, Trans and Queer Black and Brown people gave you the vanguard.

The year 2019 marked the 50th anniversary of the Stonewall Uprising in Greenwich Village in Manhattan, New York. The Stonewall was a bar that was created for white gay men. It was a space that routinely excluded any Black and Brown folks, especially Trans and gender non-conforming folks. But that fateful night at the Stonewall was "Drag night" so all the folks could get in, some with a little struggle but we digress. That night was the night that Ms. Marsha P. Johnson, Silvia Rivera, Storme DeLarverie, and other BIPOC had enough of the police pushing them around. They fought back, they fought for their lives, and because of them, the white Trans and Queer folk were moved to action, too.

When you look at the photos of the now veterans of that uprising, and those who were forward in the early organizations that it birthed, they are mostly white. Very few Black and Brown people remain alive, and the ones who are still here are rarely mentioned by any larger media outlets or far-reaching organizations. This year, Marsha, Silvia, and Storme, our Black and Brown ancestors, were invoked over and over by white voices. However, the substantive truth of Black Trans and Queer lives was never included in these soundbites. This is the truth of the occupied reality we live in. We are claimed only in death, yet the violence of that death is not connected to the structures in place which caused it and perpetuate the privilege of claiming us. Marsha P. Johnson was murdered and found floating in the Hudson. As I write this, news outlets have designated 2019 the deadliest year for Trans women (Sosin 2019), and we must remain cognizant of the fact that Black, Brown, and Indigenous women have been and continue to be murdered at disproportionately higher rates than their white Trans counterparts.

This year is also momentous because it marks 400 years since the first *documented* slaver's ship touched down in what is now known as Virginia in the United States. This is before the Mayflower! Of all the 600,000 Africans who were enslaved and survived the unimaginable violence of the middle passage, of all the 12 million Africans whose bodies were commodified and brutalized throughout the Diaspora, were none identifiable to us as what we now call LGBTQIA+? Knowing the thousands of years of documented Trans and Queer lives across African continental cultures, we know the truth. That all the "slave revolts," culture keeping, code creating, spirit and conjure working, music, and way making could not have been done without some Trans and Queer involvement.

A true and committed biodiversity of move-ments, with the most marginalized of us at the center (in the lead, not just fodder for the frontlines but in the lead) can fix the disconnect between soundbites and performance. This can give those of us marginalized by the systematic state-sanctioned violence of the prison industrial complex, police, politicized borders, and factory farming a true voice. That said, what good is centering if the spaces in which we are centered are hostile (unwittingly so or not)? It is important that time and effort be put into education and acknowledgement of privileges and all that come with them be done by those who hold the most societal power so that the full burden of the spaces we lead and grow in isn't put on those of us whom you wish to center (this includes analyzing the ways in which we view nonhumans).

Marginalized folks also need spaces that are ours alone. This is not the antithesis of inclusion; instead, it facilitates healing and community in the ways we need to make our movements thrive.

A recognition of the intensely magical co-nnections of our network of liberation movements is the only way for us to survive. ***We were brought to this pivotal moment in history by the audacity of a perception of superiority.*** The way forward is not a counter but a decimation of that perception with the audacity of mindful action. We are driven not by simple compassion but by compulsion to bring *everybody* with us. My future then, is defiantly Black, defiantly Queer, radically vegan, and absolutely will never be made through good intention.

*Cited Works*

hooks, b. (2004). *The Will to Change: Men, Masculinity, and Love*. Washington Square Press.

Sosin, K. (2019). *Trans Woman's Murder in Washington Makes 2019 Deadliest Year on Record for Transgender Americans*. NewNowNext.

# 3 CONVERSATIONS WITH ACTIVISTS

What could veganism look like for someone actively working across various movements? What are some key issues related to individual activists across vegan and LGBTQIA+ movements? How does veganism strengthen our work as LGBTQIA+ activists? These are just some of the questions that came to mind while taking part in one-on-one conversations with established queer and trans vegans working in social justice spaces. Therefore, in an effort to highlight their work and continue to build bridges between all movements, the following pages focus on messages from activists working towards liberation for both human and nonhuman animals through various media and methods.

## Q: What does being a part of the LGBTQIA+ community as a vegan mean to you?

A: Jasmin Singer, Author & Podcaster

CW: date rape, gender-based violence

My first professional job was working as an actor-educator with an AIDS-awareness theater company called Nitestar, which went into inner-city schools throughout New York City and performed shows about safer sex, domestic violence, and coming out—then followed up with the students for six weeks, during which time, we actor-educators would lead workshops where we unpacked some of the inequities the kids were experiencing and honed in on how to recognize and validate the injustices and then reframe communication around gender-based violence and HIV. This was, as you can imagine, a deeply powerful experience for all of us. At the time, I identified as bisexual and vegetarian—but through my work at Nitestar, and through being exposed to the bravery of these marginalized kids who were facing parts of themselves and their preconceived notions about sexuality, gender expression, and the stigma around HIV, I began to uncover that I was living half-truths. I'm certainly not saying that people who identify as bi are disingenuous or otherwise closeted; I actually think it's quite brave to be out as bi or pansexual. But for me, during the period when I identified as bisexual, I was not yet ready to embrace my full lesbian identity.

Since art imitates life, another layer for me during this time, almost two decades ago now, when I was in my early twenties was that just as I was helping some of these kids come to terms with sexual violence they had undergone, I was facing my own date rape that had occurred a few years prior. Despite my commitment to reframing mindsets, I was not able to fully face my own sexual attack until it became a lie by omission. I learned that I needed to show up for these kids, which meant I needed to show up for myself and start to heal.

In an ironic twist, during this same time, when I was with my fellow actor-educators for our rehearsals, during breaks, I would run across the street for (what is perhaps the most disgusting food on the planet) a container of cottage cheese. I can actually point the start of my vegan journey to a moment with this gross, coagulated cheese product. I stared at the bumpy white substance and— perhaps for the first time—I realized it was a product of gender-based violence, since dairy cows are repeatedly inseminated so that we humans can take their milk (and the male steers have their semen forcibly extracted as well). At the time, I had long introduced myself as "a vegetarian but not the mean kind," and yet the closer I got to dealing with my date rape—and the more authentic I became with these kids who were boldly confronting personal and societal biases about what it means to identify as LGBTQIA+—the more I was unleashing my true self as a vegan and a lesbian.

What had I been hiding until then? What, for me, were the connections? I realize now that the answer is that I was afraid that society would not accept me if I was either one of those, let alone both. I was afraid of limiting my options with food or with love interests. I saw the choice to be vegan as limiting, just as I saw the choice to come out as gay as limiting. What I later learned, of course, was that crossing over to this self-truth is not limiting at all; on the contrary, it's full of abundance and entire new worlds of choice and deep satisfaction.

During my time at Nitestar, I met my first vegan—a friend of a friend—and I see now the power of being out and being seen, because having her in my life normalized veganism, making it less of a stigma and more of an inroad to a community and a deep-seated truth. This is a similar story to so many otherwise closeted kids who grow up knowing one or just a few queer people; even their presence can be a guiding light, proof that there's a place for everyone. This vegan I knew was unapologetic about her worldview and quickly took me under her wing.

The sudden understanding that the dairy and egg products I had been eating ever since I ditched meat as a teenager—claiming, simply, that it was "icky"—were rooted in an oppressive system so toxic that even now, 17 years into my veganism, I continue to find new threads of injustice in its path of destruction, was life-changing. This new-to-me knowledge was as shocking as it ultimately was liberating. I was coming of age, learning how to be an autonomous adult, and suddenly being a part of a community of vegans—thanks to my new friend who opened up a whole new world to me—was a vitally important part of my process. And through this new vegan world, I met a handful of queer people who were working at the intersection of animal rights and LGBTQIA+ rights, and it was in that overlapping space that I truly found myself and my calling both personally and as an activist. Discovering my own deep-seated truth of identifying as a vegan lesbian was the first time in my life I felt my ethics were aligned with my self-expression and my true identity. Understanding that, and then celebrating it, changed everything. It was only when I embraced the personal that I turned a lens on the political, and the connections between veganism and LGBTIA+ liberation solidified even further.

Last year, I was interviewed by the European blog, "The Vegan Rainbow Project." I was asked about some of my earliest articles that made the connections between the animal rights and LGBTQIA+ movements. This is what I said: One of my first published print articles—"Coming out for Animals" from *Satya Magazine*, which I wrote in 2006—was all about the connections between LGBTQIA+ and animal rights. It pointed to the commonalities between the mindset of the oppressors of queer people and animals alike ("insert-the-blank is here for my use," "I am better than insert-the-blank," "God, or the bible, said I should bully this animal/gay person"). The final line of the article is, "Sliced to death is sliced to death, whether a slaughterhouse worker or a homophobic bully happens to be holding the knife." When I wrote that, I was spending time talking with and learning from longtime activist pattrice jones, who had been writing and thinking about those connections (and many other connections between social justice issues) for a long time, and she—as well as the other activists I interviewed for that piece—were instrumental in my early mindset as an intersectional activist. I came to the animal rights movement by way of the AIDS-awareness movement and ultimately saw each issue as a different spoke on the same wheel, which, to this day, has informed the way I approach my writing, thinking, activism, and media-making.

The feedback I received back then was mostly positive within the animal rights communities though people outside of the animal rights co-mmunities were somewhat perplexed by the parallels. However, I have noticed that since then, things have shifted within animal rights circles, and, these days, inclusivity within the animal rights movement is sparse and still taboo. In the wake of the ways the #MeToo movement has impacted the animal rights community, I have hope that our movement will continue to evolve toward equity for all individuals (human and non). With more and more media outlets reporting on injustice through a holistic lens, I also have hope that how we treat animals will also be part of the dialogue when it comes to social justice issues at large. More recently, the organization I co-founded, Our Hen House, produced a video entitled "Coming Out for Animal Rights" which speaks to many of these connections.

The overlapping issues, mindsets, dialogues, and communities between these two spaces— LGBTQIA+ and animal rights—has become my life's anchor, and, I hope, my life's work.

*Q: As a nonbinary/queer vegan, what do
sanctuaries mean to you, and how does your own
involvement with sanctuaries and nonhuman
rescue strengthen your work towards social justice
as a whole?*

A: Z. Griffler, *The Open Sanctuary Project*

The idea of starting an animal sanctuary of my own someday had inexplicably etched itself into my vague plans for the future within a few weeks of my transition into veganism. Today, I couldn't tell you what that imagined sanctuary might've looked like in my daydreams, and considering I had never so much as visited an animal sanctuary's website, let alone having ever visited a sanctuary in person, and considering at the time I was too squeamish to trim a six pound cat's nails out of fear of drawing blood, to say I was perhaps a bit out of my depth of experience would be polite.

Until the first day that I actually got involved in sanctuary work, I, like many others I know, assumed everything that took place at animal sanctuaries would be uncomplicated both logistically and ideologically. "Maybe the cows would be like giant dogs" was about as much as I had thought about most things related to farmed animals outside of my adoration for them on an abstract level.

Within my first day of actually working at a sanctuary, I quickly learned I was wrong about pretty much everything I had assumed about them. A lot of time has passed since then, and I'm still learning.

When you strip away the varnish, sanctuaries exist for the residents to live out their lives in peace, the survivors of both personal and structural trauma given the freedom to be in their bodies without anything being asked of them. In this one particular way, likely the way most folks think and talk about them, sanctuaries are indeed relatively uncomplicated.

But it would be an incomplete picture to leave it at that.

Sanctuaries are paradoxically spaces of both liberation and involuntary confinement. The residents are given more consideration than nearly any other member of their species on the planet, but there will always be significant restrictions on how they live, who they spend time with, and what they can and cannot do. There will be choices made for them by humans (sometimes gut-wrenching ones) that they don't understand, appreciate, nor can they often consent to.

To me, grappling with this ethical complexity greatly outweighs the alternative. When you look at the numbers, every farmed animal who has ever gotten out of their prescribed fate and found their way to sanctuary around the world has won the Powerball. It's one thing to know that. It's quite another to see it.

I've experienced what tens of thousands of starving, abandoned baby chickens in a freezing warehouse look, sound, and smell like. What the dead and dying feel like underfoot. Most of all, I remember the contrast between the mundanity of their pleasant agrarian surroundings and the bleak, indescribable hell of their short lives. The few individuals who made it out alive live in a comparative paradise (human-inflicted congenital health issues aside), but a couple hundred survivors stand in for the nearly 40,000 who weren't so lucky in that same row of warehouses. This exact scenario plays out far more often than I can bear to imagine.

More likely than not, that very row of bankrupted warehouses I was standing in have already been resold and filled to the brim with 40,000 more lives who were subsequently killed almost a dozen times by now.

However, this isn't a story about those chickens; it's a story about the impact of stories.

When humans (even vegan humans) visit a sanctuary, often they arrive expecting to look at anonymous farmed animals in the same manner that one's attention may drift to a hastily arranged petting zoo at a farmer's market. It's an activity to do, maybe a new profile picture to be gained.

To many folks' surprise, they can't help but meet individuals, nonhuman people with histories, personalities, preferences, and sometimes a touch of sass.

They meet a rooster whose first 41 days of life included abandonment, starvation, salvation, intensive medical care, and who now particularly enjoys wiggling contentedly in a certain dust bath with a southern exposure. They meet a pig whose story was one of rescue from indescribable daily violence, an individual who now immediately flops to her side when a human enters her area, grunting with a trusting staccato patience in hopes of yet another round of belly rubs. Maybe they don't quite meet a llama, but they do see him lounging out in a distant field, living life comfortably within the boundaries he's set.

Very often, these experiences stow away with visitors and help them confront the old stories they've held onto from a young age without ever knowing it, the ones which conclude there's such a thing as "too many" questions.

The ones that suggest they shouldn't look deeper at the systems they've accepted as "normal" at best, "regrettable, yet unalterable, so frown slightly and move on with your day," at worst.

To my surprise, sanctuaries helped dismantle some old stories that I had been unknowingly holding onto as well, and I had no idea how trans-formative this would be.

By serving individuals who had previously been an abstraction, and by witnessing solutions (however imperfect) being implemented each day by a dedicated community to provide relief from the harms carried out against them, I unlearned myths I had long accepted as truth, the ones about my own lack of agency (and therefore responsibility) when it came to helping to address other systems of oppression in the world.

Sanctuary experiences taught me that, while it is crucial to actively continue learning about issues impacting communities who have been marginalized and to be supportive of equitable change whenever possible, we as individuals have enormous power if we take action beyond passive support. We can do so much more than we ever imagined possible when we put on some muck boots and work on tangible solutions that directly support communities every single day. I've taken that perspective, forged from the ashes of well-meaning politics but what-can-I-do slacktivism, and I've brought it back to my work for other communities wherever I can in the past few years.

When not serving the animal sanctuary community, I've expanded my advocacy for the queer community, primarily the trans community. That advocacy takes many actionable forms, but at the heart of it, I use the other major lesson gained from my sanctuary work: to get people to recognize individuals, including many people like me, beyond the exhausting assumptions and stereotypes ingrained into the cultural zeitgeist. Beyond the old stories.

When each day you serve individuals who have been stripped of both their agency and their ability to vocalize in any manner that will be respected and who have no right to their very lives, you can begin to see patterns of how similar oppressions play out against community after community. Similar stories told, similar excuses made. Similar violence rendered with similar justification. And hopefully, upon truly grappling with some of the old stories you might still be carrying, you can find tools to help in the fight for the liberation of all oppressed communities.

One fight inspires the other, which inspires yet another. They're all the same fight.

FELIZ BRUECK AND McNEILL

**Q: *Working together across movements (anti-racism, LGBTQIA+, and vegan) and decentering nonhumans in the process is a big concern for vegans, how does ensuring that we create safe spaces for all actually help center nonhumans in their own movement?***

A: Michelle Carrera, *Chilis on Wheels*

When I first went vegan in 2001, I was 21 years old and living in the town of Mayaguez, Puerto Rico, where I mostly grew up. I didn't know about factory farms or egg hatcheries, and the local health food stores sold very little appealing products. I had never heard the word vegan and was even one of those people that pronounced it *vay-gahn*. I had seen the person in my pet rooster, Piolin, the way he liked cuddles, the way he responded to his name and waddled over when called, and seeing him no different than a dog, or a cat, or a human was enough to give up the consumption of all sentient people. As in most cases, the more I found resources on vegetarianism and veganism, the more I started resenting humans. And I fell into the mainstream vision of what activism should look like. I, however, lived in Puerto Rico, and thus, I relied on poorly translated materials shipped in the mail by some of the big animal rights orgs.

The more I read about the personhood project, the more I read about the great apes and how genetically closely related to us they are, and this idea that we should give non-humans the same rights as humans made me question *whose rights* they were referring to. This took me down the path of political radicalization. I was already a young out queer, disillusioned by the strict gender roles inherent in the middle class I grew up in and well aware of the colonization that the people in the island I grew up in was forced to endure. Although I lacked the proper language to articulate this, my queerness, my veganism, my other identities all stemmed from a rejection of capitalism, and its repression of freedom. My quest became a yearning to understand and experience liberation.

As soon as I moved to NYC in 2004, I joined the local nonhuman animal rights activist scene. Shortly thereafter, in part because of my expanding political views, and in part because I didn't feel like I was allowed to bring all parts of myself into my activism, I hesitantly eventually withdrew from the movement. I went on to do activist work on other human issues, and each time, I felt like I had to compartmentalize some part of myself and prioritize one identity at the expense of my other ones.

Within the nonhuman animal rights movement, we are very intentional in spelling out the wholeness of our experience by using the terms "human and nonhuman animals," implying we are part of a continuum, we are not separate, and our experience is the same. However, this concept often stops at our language, and our work hardly reflects these values when we consider the human as part of that group of animals that deserves rights and liberation. Our oppressions are all connected and stem from the same white supremacist, patriarchal, colonial settler capitalist system, and because our oppressions are not fragmented, neither can our approach.

Our oppressions manifest in similar and yet different ways. In all cases, it involves silencing, invisibility, discarding, commodification, objectify-cation. Queer folks, People of Color, Black folks, working class folks, Nonhuman folks, we are all kept from our fullness, from our authenticity, indoctri-nated to believe we are lesser than, that we are inherently wrong, and yet one purchase away from freedom. This is upheld through popular culture, schooling, and legal systems and policed by each other.

In all of my work through Chilis on Wheels, Casa Vegana de la Comunidad, The Microsanctuary Re-source Center, and other projects, (and my personal

Unschooling parenting, Minimalist embodiment), I have searched for liberation, emotional, spiritual, practical, concrete liberation, and am still searching. Who are we underneath all the trauma and oppression? And how can we find a defining answer when our selves are always changing and when the tactics of our oppressors keep shifting and changing and disguising themselves? I have come to believe that liberation is not a state but a practice, and we can never reach a definition, but we have to address it in whole.

I approach subjects holistically. What this means in practice is that we need to have all aspects of our struggles present at once, in whichever ratio it manifests. In life, but especially in doing community work and liberation work, the ability to be radically authentic is crucial in building honest, loyal, longstanding relationships. Building these relationships is the purpose of our work.

Just as we cannot compartmentalize our identities in community building, we cannot compartmentalize our ideas or our approaches in our work. This is how and why my work touches, interacts, and builds bridges with other social justice movements, to destroy the compartmentalization that single-issue work brings. Colonization broke us into different pieces, and we need to seek ways in which we can be made whole again.

At our Casa Vegana de la Comunidad in Puerto Rico, for example, we hold weekly workshops on a variety of topics, from vegan cooking classes, fitness workshops, sustainability, upcycling projects, collecting rainwater, to talks on decolonization, cli-mate change, herbalism, to community events such as documentary nights, and community nights. Whatever the reason people have for walking up to our community center, the first people they meet are Silencio and Julia, our two resident rescued chickens. Paintings of typically farmed animals in freedom adorn our walls, and pamphlets on nonhuman animal liberation (not just on plant-based eating) are found in our information corner. Anyone walking into our center, whether coming in for a sustainability workshop or because they're curious about the health benefits of a plant-based diet, are immediately confronted with nonhuman animals and are given a chance to make an emotional bond with these very lively chicken people. Visitors are also always fed vegan snacks or a vegan meal and can take one of our postcards with a recipe for our delicious chili. There is never a fee for attending these events although we encourage bringing in a vegan food item, at least one can of vegetables. This way, we can keep our projects going, and there is a true community investment in the project as well.

Approaching our oppressions from whole parts allows us to have maximum reach. And rather than preaching to people, we simply structure our programs in a way that is holistic and all-encompassing.

The other facet of my work is to make, maintain, and sustain relationships within other social justice movements and struggles. Our Chilis on Wheels (CoW) chapters, which are decentralized and led by the communities they serve, regularly collaborate with other social justice organizations and struggles because the organizers themselves are part of those struggles. In Puerto Rico, CoW served meals to the people in the successful protests to oust our corrupt governor and collected and provided supplies to the medics for the front lines; continuously serves meals to the People's Assemblies popping up around the island; and collaborates with agro-ecology projects and a queer feminist environmental group leading a community center in Santurce. Similarly, in Hawaii, Chilis on Wheels Maui served meals and created a hydrating station to the protectors of Mauna Kea and regularly participates in community events regarding food insecurity and land sovereignty. In our New York Chapter, we regularly bring snacks to diverse movement protests held in the parks that we serve and collaborate with other organizations sharing our food resources.

Solidarity work is important because it builds bridges between the people in different social justice movements. This allows us all to have a stake in collective liberation to build those trusted relationships that will allow us to have a stronger front against oppressive forces. It allows us to build bigger, more expansive, stronger, communities. The stronger a community is, the better a chance it has to resist and thrive.

Community is interdependence. It's pooling our resources and skills together to survive with the hope that we will eventually thrive. It's acknowledging that we have different skills and different sets of capital to offer each other. It's learning together and sharing of ourselves, holding each other accountable in growth, and supporting one another. Building a shared vision of liberation that we can grow towards and work on together.

There are no saviors, just us. Us, sharing our food, our shelter, our resources, the bits of information we've learned and gathered along the way, our ways of experiencing the world among each other. Our contribution is food, but sometimes it isn't. Sometimes it's offering coats in the winter, distributing warm gloves. Sometimes it's accompanying an elder on a supermarket visit. Sometimes our contribution is organizing, planning, structuring.

Sometimes it's holding a sign in a protest, adding a body to a march, a loud voice to a chant. Sometimes it's sharing truths we've learned. Sometimes it's upholding other voices. Sometimes it's upholding the work of a member of our community that is being pushed back on. Some-times it's putting the force of our connections behind a targeted community, standing up for each other, by each other, together.

This work is not easy. It comes at such a high personal expense. We must be willing to sacrifice without falling into martyrdom. We must remain open and empathic while learning not to carry other people's suffering. We must be willing to be flexible while remaining in authenticity. We must be willing to change the tone while standing by our message. We must learn to navigate conflict when it arises, and it inevitably does, especially the larger the community grows. We must be willing to hold space for others when they need it and to request it when we do.

We cannot depend on a system that is out to get us, so we have to depend on each other, depend on what we are able to organize for ourselves – our libraries and tool sharing, our meal shares, our community gardens, our knowledge, our defenses, and our medics. We are resisting further encroaching, further colonization. So, my work with

Chilis on Wheels is not so much the meal, although sometimes it is, but the relationships we build among each other so that we can build and resist collectively, for all of us animals.

The Microsanctuary Resource Center, which provides resources for people leading micro-sanctuaries, has a recurring grant for Micro-sanc-tuaries of Color, established in collaboration with Sanctuary Publishers, to ensure that People of Color from all over the world who are leading or want to create micro sanctuaries can access resources often denied to them from other sources, for the care of non-human animals, building equity within minoritized communities, and encouraging the view within all communities that nonhuman animals can and should live among us and form part of our communities. A microsanctuary starts from the premise that our space and our resources, no matter how limited, often are still sufficient for us to provide sanctuary to individual animals RIGHT NOW in order to prevent them from ever again being used as commodities. It can be as little as one nonhuman animal not typically viewed as a companion animal, or it can be in an urban setting. And it is radical. Opening our space to people in need of sanctuary, allowing them to decolonize themselves and relearn who they are in liberation, is what we are all aspiring to. And building community, sharing learning resources, and providing access to funds among caregivers is crucial for the care of the nonhumans in our spaces and for ourselves. Opening dedicated safe(r) spaces so that marginalized people can offer that is important because in learning to see others as free, we are also creating the vision of ourselves as free. My work with the newly formed Queer Vegan Supper Club (in NYC), where queer identified folk over the age of 30+ with radical politics come together to share a vegan meal, is a perfect example of stepping out of our compartmentalization to be in community together, a space where we are free to discuss our experience and also our way forward.

Including microsanctuaries, accessibility to vegan food, community and activist support, mutual aid, access to funds, and anti-speciesist frameworks within this work helps other animals by not just making relationships with other social justice movements but working within them. And making those spaces safe(r) so that all folks can feel at home and whole while participating and making it their own can be the difference between an activist that stays for the long-run, invested in all of our struggles, or one that is forced to leave. In the latter, both the human and nonhuman animals suffer, and we are once again playing right into colonization, fracturing our beautiful selves.

**Q:** *How could the LGBTQIA+ movement and vegan movement improve and work with one another to create the most effective change in the world at this point in time?*

A: Suzy González, Artist

A common thread between LGBTQIA+ movements and vegan movements is the concept of non-violence. Violence from the white heteropatriarchy, both historically and in the present day, affects both queer communities and non-human animals. How can we only believe in non-violence for some?

As a queer Xicana vegan living in San Antonio, TX, I see further definite overlaps between LGBTQIA+ and vegan movements; I also see a common resistance for them to overlap. There are many people that assume incorrectly that traditional Mexican food must contain meat or dairy. There is also an unfortunate amount of heteropatriarchal-siding citizens within the state of Texas.

Although seemingly disconnected, I see these two observations as intrinsically tied in the same way that the communities that oppose these notions also have tight links. For example, the local self-publishing zine community is typically a radically-leaning queer-safe space, but it is not predominately vegan. There are often gender-neutral bathrooms, pronouns on name-tags, and queer content in the work. Usually, there will be a vegan food option at these gatherings. However, it is rare that these are the majority. As an artist and organizer, it can be disappointing when events that I participate in do not offer vegan options, especially in a time when there is an awareness of intersecting oppressions that include human and nonhuman animal exploitation such as animal agriculture-led climate catastrophe.

While my desire is to hold organizers account-table for having non-violent food options, I also recognize the truths behind food desserts and the all-too-common lack of accessibility to organic, fresh produce combatting with the affordability of meat and dairy options. In fact, San Antonio ranked No. 71 of 100 U.S. cities in 2019 ranking vegetarian-friendliness (Thompson 2019). While accessibility is a definite issue, we have to be honest that this is not an issue for the most privileged within our own communities. In addition, as has been supported by organizations, such as the Academy of Nutrition and Dietetics, what we consume will likely affect our communities health-wise and could potentially save on future medical bills. Offering more vegan options at community events will help foster a space whereas many forms of anti-oppression work can be represented, including veganism, but it will also create a more health-conscious spread that all of our community can enjoy.

It's a somewhat different experience to attend a Veg Fest and a Pride event. Unfortunately, both are tied to consumer capitalism and they seem to be "trending." However, they both provide spaces where either vegans or queer folx can feel somewhat safer. But what about the intersections of a queer vegan Person of Color? Vegan and Pride movements, despite their origins, are still tied to whiteness. Until we all recognize that people do not exist within single issue identities, we can't progress either movement. Queer theory often denies a feminine/masculine social binary, veganism denies the human/animal divide, and being a Brown person falls within the Black/white binary. I know that I am both feminine and masculine, both human and animal, and racially mixed. I believe in the idea of both/and rather than either/or.

With regards to mestizaje, Gloria Anzaldúa (1999) claimed that "the answer to the problem between the white race and the colored, between males and females, lies in healing the split that originates in the very foundation of our lives, our culture, our languages, our thoughts. A massive uprooting of dualistic thinking in the individual and collective consciousness is the beginning of a long struggle, but one that could, in our best hopes, bring us to the end of rape, of violence, of war." White supremacy enforced dualistic thinking gives us permission to assign hierarchical value to identity groups, and we must realize that human supremacy reigning over the entirety of the animal kingdom is no different. When it comes to queer veganism of color, rejecting dualistic thought that runs deep in our colonial culture may just be the answer to non-violence across the board.

If People of Color, those of us whose ancestors experienced violent colonization, are working to decolonize or re-indigenize aspects of our lives, we cannot leave out diet, gender, and sexuality. As we seek to replenish our ancestral queerness, we may also look into the concept of decolonizing diet or reclaiming the plant-based foods of our ancestors. In it, Calvo explains, *"Decolonize Your Diet* begins with the premise that we are living with the legacy of over 500 years of colonization of the Americas ...Colonization meant a transfer of land from Native peoples to Europeans, the death of millions of Indigenous people, the rape of Native women, and the violent suppression of Indigenous languages, religions, and cultures (2015)." There are reasons why many Tejanos think of traditional Mexican food as containing flour tortillas, fajitas, barbacoa, cheese, pan dulce, *y más*. Pre-colonial foods "were among the healthiest foods on the planet and...

many of the less healthy aspects of Mesoamerican cuisine came about as a direct result of colonization—with the introduction of wheat, beef, cheese, cooking oils, and sugar."[3] These foods are post-colonial in nature. In harnessing our ancestral memory, we recall that food is medicine and that it's meant to provide nourishment rather than illness. Along with the colonization of consumption came the colonization of sexuality and gender identity, one that persists today. As Gruen and jones argue, "In the Americas, culturally condoned expressions of same-sex sexuality were so common among Indigenous peoples that this was frequently cited by invading Europeans as justification for cultural genocide (2014)." Queerness is still seen as deviant, and those whose identities and appearances perform further from heteronormativity are more at risk of violence. Whereas a multitude of genders existed, and still do for Indigenous peoples, Christian setter colonialist society insisted on a binaristic view. However, things are changing.

There is a beautiful restaurant and bar in San Antonio called *La Botanica* that is queer women-run and is entirely vegan. I know that, when I go there, I'm in a safe space for many reasons. Making space for queerness and veganism to exist simultaneously without fear of violence is so important to our collective well-being. When we consider the work of

Carol J. Adams and we see that veganism can be a way to deny patriarchy, it makes sense that queer spaces be vegan spaces. The nonhuman animal rights movement can often feel uninformed on human rights. However, the same is true for the LGBTQIA+ movement. Rather than have tunnel vision on a very specific cause, we must all consider the intersections and complexities of identity. To put it simply, we must work on a variety of topics, with intertwined movements, if we want to decolonize our lives and work towards a more compassionate and equitable future.

*Cited Works*

Thompson, L. (2019). San Antonio Ranks Among the Least Vegan- and Vegetarian-Friendly U.S. Cities. *San Antonio Current*: www.sacurrent.com/ Flavor/archives/2019/09/30/san-antonio-ranks-among-the-least-vegan-and-vegetarian-friendly-us-cities.

Anzaldúa, G. (1999). *Borderlands: The New Mestiza La Frontera*. Aunt Lute Books.

Calvo, L. and Esquibel, C.R. (2015). *Decolonize Your Diet: Plant-Based Mexican American Recipes for Health and Healing*. Arsenal Pulp.

Gruen, L. and jones, p. (2014). Eros and the
Mechanisms of Eco-Defense. in Carol J. Adams (ed),
*Ecofeminism: Feminist Intersections with Other
Animals & the Earth*. Bloomsbury.

FELIZ BRUECK AND McNEILL

## *Q: How do plant-based diets and veganism help you, a two-spirit woman, decolonize?*

A: Margaret Robinson, Scholar

I see a strong connection between gender, food, and decolonization, both historically and in a contemporary setting.

Indigenous cultures in North America certainly had genders, and many consider some of those genders to be more accommodating of difference than a binary Western framework. But we should avoid generalizing across nations since some First Nations had very rigid binary genders while others had multiple genders and a more fluid approach.

The Anishinaabemowin gender term "Agokwe" is recorded in settler documents from 1830 written by John Tanner, an interpreter reporting on his experiences among the Anishinaabe (Robinson 2019). Two-spirit author Nathan Adler explains that in Anishinaabemowin, "egwa" means "and" and "kwe" means "girl," so "Agokwe" may literally mean "and-woman" (Niigan Noodin Adler 2014). How-ever, gender expressions change over time, so what it meant to be agokwe in 1830 and what it means to be agokwe today may be very different.

Colonial authorities intentionally destroyed Indigenous gender systems and erased language fluency. Settler governments and churches forcibly confined children in residential or boarding schools where they were re-gendered into binary Western categories. So, they cut their hair and forced them to dress and act in ways that conformed to European gender roles, and they also forced them to adopt Christianity, which declared those gender roles as ordained by God. These schools forced students to speak only English (or in some regions, only French), which eliminated Indigenous vocabulary for gender. So instead of having positive Indigenous term to describe their gender, people were forced to use English labels, some of which, like "sodomite," carried very negative connotations. Those schools operated for 175 years in Canada and 100 years in the United States, and they did enormous damage to individuals and their descendants and to their cultures.

Part of the colonial process focused on changing Indigenous food practices. Colonial governments forced Indigenous men to farm instead of hunt. This was intended to eliminate migratory patterns among those First Nations who followed migrating animals across their territory, or who shifted from summer hunting grounds to winter hunting grounds (like my people, the Mi'kmaq, did). Of course, not all First Nations were migratory. Some farming nations stayed put, building villages, towns, and cities, and some farmed and also hunted migratory animals like the buffalo. In many nations—such as the Tsalagi (Cherokee), the Lakȟóta, or the Diné (Navajo)—farming was traditionally a woman's activity. So, when colonial authorities embarked on a plan to convert First Nations men into farmers, women were forced out of farming as men were forced in. I can't imagine the loss of traditional farming knowledge that must have entailed or the damage it must have done to people's gendered sense of self. Therefore, I see a strong connection between gender, food, and decolonization.

If we're going to decolonize—to undo the damage done to our nations—we need to examine what happened, how it impacted gender, language, and food practices and consider how to move forward. Decolonizing isn't about simply returning to traditional practices (although sometimes it's that too); it's about figuring out how to live traditional values in contemporary settings.

My own nation, the Mi'kmaq, didn't farm in the way Europeans did. Women were traditionally gatherers of cultivated plant food. Therefore, some of our territory contained intentionally cultivated "wild" plants. Some of what I try to do as an Indigenous vegan woman is re-learn what those plants were and how to gather and prepare them. I'm particularly fond of ma'sus, or fiddleheads (the early frond of the Ostrich Fern), sautéed in a bit of garlic.

Although tradition is important, for me, expressing a two-spirit gender isn't about mimicking the past. It's about how to incorporate meaningful aspects of our culture into daily life. Sometimes that's spiritual like figuring out how to show respect for the other animals that share our territory. Sometimes it's literal like learning from a knowledge keeper what's edible and how to prepare and serve it.

*Cited Works*

Robinson, M. (2019). Two-Spirit Identity in a Time of Gender Fluidity. *Journal of homosexuality*. DOI: 10.1080/00918369.2019.1613853

Niigan Noodin Adler, N. (2014). Two Spirit. Goodreads author blog: https://www.goodreads.com/author_blog_posts/9545643-two-spirit-originally-published-as-reclaiming-two-spirit-in-issue-25 Originally published as Nathan Niigan Noodin Adler (2013) Reclaiming Two-Spirit. *Shameless Magazine* (25).

**Q:** *Why should LGBTQIA+ and vegan communities work together to fight intersecting oppressions?*

A: Lilia Trenkova, *Collectively Free*

When communities work together, magic happens. Whether we are organizing or building connections, the sharing of time and space in cooperation brings an exchange in energy and experiences, which in turn can spark new ideas and new work. Cooperation is the foundation of resilience and a coming together in power, to challenge existing systems and build new ones. So, to paraphrase the question posed—how can LGBTQIA+ and vegan communities cooperate better? What can each community bring to the other, and what can come out of it that is both pro-animal and pro-queer?

No matter where in the world, there's a strong social stigmatization of (that easily tips into violence against) queer sexuality and gender variance beyond the assigned binary as "animalistic," "uncivilized," and "impure." This a result of colonization and still persists in both colonized and colonizer countries. So much of what we learn in school, too, about our own anatomy and behavior as well as that of animals has been based on colonizer science and cisgender, heterosexual,

Christian, white male bias. This bias still dominates the field of sciences. We have yet to see a nature documentary free of it, for example, where animals are portrayed as having relationships with one another beyond the purposes of procreation or competition.

The animal world is so gloriously queer! (See below for some book recommendations on this.) The queer community can find much affirmation through deeper connections with non-humans. A deeper look into the animal world shows not only how common and natural queerness is—and how there's nothing wrong with it and us—but also that queerness plays an integral part in the thriving of any species' societies. In other words, not only do queer animals exist, they are needed in their communities. How empowering if queer people were to internalize this instead of the self-hatred imposed on us by the cis/hetero mainstream?

Vegans, and especially those involved in animal rights, liberation, and caregiving, can also enrich and strengthen their anti-speciesism work through an appreciation of animal queerness. A queered look into personhood shows us how to see and appreciate someone for who they are even when we may not relate to their behavior or desires. A queered look into animal personhood lets us see animals beyond their species as people, people with determination and agency. This can be a humbling and growing experience that can counteract the toxic human savior complex that permeates animal liberation/rescue circles, where words like "voiceless" and "helpless" actually dishonor animals' determination and agency.

A queered look into animal oppression shows that animals are exploited not only because of their species but also because of their sexes and sexualities. For example, farmed dairy cows are reduced down to how much milk their glands can generate; the bulls used to impregnate them are reduced down to how well their DNA continues the lineage of these cows. Both are denied personhood, and that includes an expression of their sexuality. A few years back there was the story of Benjy, a bull who showed no interest in the cows but rather in the other bulls. His queerness was bad for the farm's business and that was enough to get him marked for slaughter; a gay bull has no purpose, and thus no right, to live. He was lucky to get the attention of animal rights activists, and he was able to go to a sanctuary instead. Benjy's is a story that we know of...but how many farmed animals ever get to experience this level of personal awareness?

So, what can come out of a cooperation between LGBTQIA+ and vegan communities? More queer vegans, sure, but also an ever more expansive queer liberation and animal liberation movements. A queer liberation movement that centers people's autonomy and right to exist however their queerness manifests—not one that centers conformity to the cis/hetero mainstream. An animal liberation movement that centers animals' autonomy and right to exist how they wish. A total liberation movement that centers cooperation and mutual empowerment.

\*\*\*

## Lilia's Suggestions
## for Further Readings and Thoughts

Books that explore animal queerness:

*Biological Exuberance: Animal Homosexuality and Natural Diversity* by Bruce Bagemihl

*Evolution's Rainbow: Diversity, Gender and Sexuality in Nature and People* by Joan Roughgarden

*Queer Ecologies: Sex, Nature, Politics, Desire* by Catriona Mortimer-Sandilands

On the human savior complex:

*Savior Complexes and Animal Justice Work* from the
blog *Chickpeas and Change*

Protest actions that address violence against
nonhumans animals and LGBTQIA+ humans:

*Collectively Free*'s disruptions of Chick-fil-A

*Collectively Free*'s Pride March demos

## Q: As a Black Queer vegan, how do you feel you are treated by the LGBTQIA+ and mainstream vegan movements?

A: Ikora Rey, *The Black Queer Vegan Diaries*

Many folks erase people like me when they say "veganism is 'problematic'" because of racism, ableism, etc. Yet, here I am – a Black, Queer, Gendervague, Neurodivergent vegan very much aware of their compounded identities and oppressions while firmly committed to this concept named "veganism."

But what is veganism really? To me, it's about how I view the world. It's a mindset. It's the belief that nonhumans are deserving of the same rights as humans.

Do I believe we all get those rights or not? No, none of us are granted these rights.

When I say "us," I mean all of us who aren't "the default human," white able-bodied cis man with money, etc. Veganism will neither fix nor detriment the ability for us to fight against oppression of almost all humans. It's a thought process by which we understand the true size of the group who is oppressed and clearly articulate that the scope of oppression also includes nonhumans, and that as humans, we experience advantages that are unearned over nonhuman animals.

Truthfully, we rely on these advantages for our lives to be enhanced. We, vegans like myself, believe that this is not the best case. So, we seek to reduce our impact as much as we can.

What does this mean? We don't just choose to die by refusing to take our medications (which was tested on animals by law); we won't just kill ourselves because the existence of human society is causing the deaths of nonhumans. NO! This doesn't mean people who can't "be vegan" should be shunned. The appearance of being vegan while still harming nonhumans in ways that we cannot control is not the point. The point is that in a very non-vegan world, veganism isn't about perfection. One can be vegan while admitting how imperfect we are and allowing ourselves to improve as best we can. When we have a choice, we choose the path with the least harm. When we do not have a choice, we advocate and work on root issues like accessibility.

As a metaphor for this:

It's like how one basic part of Christianity religion is that "all have sinned and fall short of the glory of god." This means Christians believe sin exists. They believe sin is a uniquely human trait. They believe sin is bad and should be reduced. They believe they should do their best to minimize sin in their lives and the lives of others. They believe sin will still occur. They believe sin will still occur, AND the sinner is still a Christian. They believe Christianity is accepting the truth as presented by the Bible and then taking steps to minimize sin. It's the same with veganism. I don't try to harm non-humans, but by the definition of veganism, I am admitting that I sometimes do. It's inevitable when their exploitation has been so deeply interwoven in our everyday lives. However, like I mentioned, this comes down to the choices we make when we can.

Therefore, for me, my ability to "be vegan" (I would actually call this ability to minimize harm – always vegan) is based on my capabilities and reach as a human. I can eliminate animal products from my diet. I can avoid buying animal tested products except my medicine. I can avoid exploitation of animals in zoos, racing, etc. there's a lot I can do. I do all of those things, but there's a lot I can't. It's hypocritical and wrong to determine one's vegan status solely based on their abilities. It's also wrong to say veganism is problematic for saying everyone can be vegan because it's true. Everyone can. It's about accepting the truth and your sincere intent to reduce harm.

FELIZ BRUECK AND McNEILL

# 4 A FINAL NOTE

Julia Feliz Brueck

While the international voices in this book all have different birth places, journeys, and experiences that have shaped who we are, we queer and trans vegans are indeed connected through the realization that our identities as marginalized people empowered us to take a stance beyond ourselves. We do so consistently and across each and every social justice community we have the power to do so.

Nonhuman exploitation guides and supports so much of the oppression that still persists to this day that it is indeed a duty to recognize our human privilege when it comes knocking at our door. So, we pose the following question to you: what does it mean to accomplish liberation through consistent anti-oppression?

It means that our work towards liberation must be collectively addressed across movements and species. Single-issue activism is no longer relevant, nor efficient; this is clear as so many interco-nnections remain ignored and unaddressed in a supremacist society that benefits from our inability to recognize this. What is liberation for those with the most privilege when those with the least are still oppressed? How can we celebrate marriage equality when our Black and Brown trans sisters are disproportionally targeted and murdered compared to the rest of us? How can we feel accomplished in our fight while our queer Siblings-of-Color, half a world away, continue to experience compounding struggles because they are still bound by outdated colonial laws that are still enforced on them? How can we celebrate our achievements as a movement over meals made up of the abused bodies of the very nonhumans used to erase and condemn us for our queerness and transness? How can we ignore all the little ways that supremacist ideology has been passed down and continues to be reproduced? We cannot – even when we are untouched directly by it. This is what binds our commitment to one ano-ther under consistent anti-oppression.

As Black Queer political activist and educator Angela Davis explained, "Sometimes you have to struggle to understand the interrelationships and connectedness of things that are clearly connected." This struggle is real and never-ending in our quest to actively oppose our privileges and to use them to counter our own hand in the oppression of others. Long gone are the days in which our understanding of identities different to our own and even our own as queer and trans individuals are compartmentalized. In essence, if you walk away with anything from this anthology, let it be the understanding that oppressions are interconnected and to fight for queer liberation you must also fight for nonhuman animal liberation, and beyond.

# 5 ABOUT THE CONTRIBUTORS

**LoriKim Alexander** is originally from Kingston, Jamaica. She has dedicated her life to working for social and environmental justice specifically organizing around justice for LGBTQIA+ Black, Brown, and Indigenous Communities. LoriKim's work in anthropology and as a trained biologist has facilitated her in centering initiatives against environmental racism as well as the implementation of environmental education for People of Color around Indigenous ecological knowledge and deco-lonialism through veganism for the past 25 years. Currently, she is the Co-Director of BlackCuse Pride, an organization dedicated to building unified, empowered, and fully reflected Queer and Trans Black Indigenous Communities. Having lived in different parts of the US for three decades, LoriKim now resides in NYC where she continues her work as a facilitator and organizer in an effort to ensure the creation of spaces that center the most marginalized.

**Grayson Black** is ardent about food justice, sustainability, and human and non-human animal liberation. Given their passion, Grayson is an International Studies major with a concentration in Social Justice at Virginia Commonwealth University and, presently, at the University of Edinburgh. Grayson is also a triple minor in French, history, and political science with the goal of reaching a holistic approach in their future scholastic and occupational endeavors. They are a journalist for their University's Global Education newsletter and has received inductions into the National Leadership Honors Society and the National French Honors Society. Outside of University, Grayson has also worked for Vegan Action, an international animal rights nonprofit.

**Moe Constantine** grew up in Bakersfield, California and recently completed a Bachelor's of Arts in Food Justice and Film at Bard College at Simon's Rock. He is currently finishing his Master's of Arts in Critical Sociology at Brock University, where he is part of the Critical Animal Studies program and helps run a community-based Reproductive Justice activist group. His Master's research focuses on the environmental justice movement in his hometown and the strategies that activists have developed to effectively navigate a politically and socially conservative context. He hopes to soon be putting much more of his time and energy toward hands-on, radical grassroots organizing and is now accepting job offers if anyone reading this should have one.

**Shiri Eisner** is an activist and writer living in Tel Aviv. Her identities include Mizrahi, bisexual, gender-queer, polyam, feminist, disabled/chronically ill, vegan, geek, and cat lady. She is the author of the Lambda-nominated book *Bi: Notes for a Bisexual Revolution*.

**Julia Feliz Brueck** is a trained conservation ecologist with undergraduate and graduate degrees in the field of science. They are also a resource activist, educator, and published illustrator. Julia is a published author and editor of community book projects such as *Veganism in an Oppressive World* and *Veganism of Color*. They also coined the term *consistent anti-oppression*, which is the path Julia follows in their activism across all social justice issues and especially with regards to veganism in an effort to ensure they address their own hand in the oppression of others while resisting their own vocally and unapologetically.

**Janine Fuentes** is a long-time vegan and nonhuman animal lover since birth. In 1994, she was finally able to break away from the expected norms of nonhuman exploitation once she understood her actions and their impact on the lives of others. Janine has since worked as a tenacious volunteer advocate for nonhuman animals while juggling a professional career and ongoing education.

**Karla Galvez** is a Salt Lake City, Utah, local. Karla is currently involved in various arenas but holds the lenses of activism and anti-oppression work dearly. When they are not working on their Nutrition degree or at UPS, they work as a personal trainer. Karla also spends their time listening to music, going to shows, enjoying art, nature, friends and family, quality time with companion animals, volunteering, working out, and more. Aside from the heavy work & philosophy that Karla enjoys, they are lighthearted, highly empathetic, friendly, alternative, gothic, silly, artsy, and a fabulous friend.

**Suzy González** is an artist, curator, zinester, educator, and community organizer. She has had solo exhibits at Presa House Gallery, Hello Studio, Palo Alto College, and a recent two-person exhibit with Eliseo Casiano at Texas A&M University Corpus Christi. Suzy co-publishes *Yes, Ma'am* zine, co-organizes the San Anto Zine Fest, and is half of the collective *Dos Mestizx.* She received a 2017 National Association of Latino Arts and Cultures (NALAC) Fund for the Arts Grant, is a 2018 alum of the NALAC Leadership Institute, and a 2019 alum of the Intercultural Leadership Institute and NYFA Immigrant Artist Mentoring Program. Suzy holds an MFA from the Rhode Island School of Design and a BFA from Texas State University. She is based in San Antonio, TX.

**Z. Griffler** is a documentary filmmaker, activist for asexual visibility and education, and the executive editor of *The Open Sanctuary Project*.

**Chris H.** is just another white English person trying daily to peel back the layers of all the violent white (!) lies we tell one another; to stay on their authentic anti-racism journey; to do less and no harm in the world; and to get out of the way of the Black people, Indigenous people, and other People of Color who are doing the real work of liberation in this world.

**Leah Kirts** is a writer based in Queens. Her expertise is grounded in connections across ecofeminism, queerness, and veganism.

**Zoie (Zane) McNeill** is a dirt queer from Appalachia fighting for y'all to really mean all. They are a genderqueer activist-scholar, socially engaged artist, and 10-year vegan passionate about consistent anti-oppression work that uplifts the most marginalized within our communities. They are currently working on a community-building project raising queer voices in Appalachia, establishing a collective guide on how to do activist scholarship / be an activist scholar, and  on the editorial support board of a forthcoming collection challenging white supremacy in the LGBT movement.

**Dr. S. Marek Muller** is a queer autistic vegan. She is also an assistant professor of communication and rhetorical studies at Florida Atlantic University. There, she teaches and researches on human rights, nonhuman animal rights, and the human/animal binary. Specifically, she critiques the rhetoric of speciesism as it is used by persons looking to exploit nonhuman animals by "animalizing" them, persons looking to exploit humans by "dehumanizing" them, and persons fighting for social/environmental justice by articulating the interconnections of human and nonhuman animal exploitation. Dr. Muller received her PhD in Communication, with a certificate in Women's & Gender Studies, from the University of Utah in 2018.

**Patti Nyman** holds a Master's degree in Social and Political Thought from York University in Toronto with a concentration in ethics and theories of liberation and is currently pursuing a Certificate in Nonprofit Management from Simon Fraser University. They have taught undergraduate courses in the social sciences, published academic articles in feminist theory and the philosophy of religion, and created the e-book *Why Veganism*. Mx. Nyman works as Campaign Director for *Animal Place*, a farmed animal sanctuary in Northern California, and is on the board of the organization *Encompass*.

**Agnieszka Olszak** is an ordinary woman fighting for nonhuman animal rights under the Open Cages Association in Poland. She is a blogger, feminist, and lesbian and believes that there is a better, more magical world out there somewhere. Agnieszka is also a book lover and a mother of three dogs, two rabbits, and a black cat.

**Doel Rakshit** is transgender by birth and vegan by choice. Doel is a vocal artist, performer, and activist based in India.

**Jocelyn "Yaya" Ramírez** (she/her), from the Humboldt Park and Logan Square 'hoods of Chicago, is committed to the liberation of all peoples including non-human animals. As a young, disabled/ neurodivergent Mexican-American fem of color, her work centers reproductive justice for oppressed youth. Yaya, a trained social worker, birth worker and aspiring healer, is passionate about cultivating practices integrating harm re-duction, community care, pleasure and healing, disability, and trans-formative justice. Although Yaya does not know her full ancestry, she believes that by healing and holding herself accountable, she will also heal and hold her ancestors accountable and be a present elder/ancestor for youth.

**Ikora Rey** is a Black, pansexual, nonbinary, fat vegan who takes an unapologetic stance on calling out injustice. They live on Kangaroo Island in a state known as South Australia. The country of their current land is unknown; however, Ikora acknowledges that they live and work on Aboriginal land. Ikora honors Aboriginal elders, past, present, and emerging. Ikora spends most of their time resisting through being alive, knowing that just having a life is a resistance to the system of white supremacy that surrounds their every day. Ikora is a natural storyteller and, through their stories, makes connections between oppression across species, gender, sexuality, and a variety of other marginalized individuals and groups. Ikora works in technology with a specific focus on mentoring and supporting People of Color and non-human animals.

**Dr. Margaret Robinson** is a two-spirit L'nu scholar from Eski'kewaq, Nova Scotia, and a member of the Lennox Island First Nation. Her work examines the impact of intersecting oppressions and draws on critical, postcolonial, and queer theories, intersectionality, and third wave feminism.

**R. S.** is a gay man born in Mumbai, India, where coming out in a society where queer people are looked down on was difficult for him, and therefore, he relocated to Toronto. R. S. hopes to one day work in the communications department of a vegan organization. One of his favorite past times is listening to his favorite artist, Raja Kumari, or reading. Currently, he is learning about Indigenous justice issues in Canada from books like *Peace and Good Order* by Harold R. Johnson.

**Brooke Shephard** is based in Austin, Texas, with her partner and dog. Brooke spends most of her time writing, reading, and taking part in nonhuman animal rights activism.

**Jasmin Singer** is the author of the memoir *Always Too Much and Never Enough* (Penguin Random House's Berkley, 2016) and *The VegNews Guide to Being a Fabulous Vegan* (Da Capo, December 2020). She is the co-host and co-founder of the long running *Our Hen House* podcast, the Senior Online Features Editor for *VegNews*, and the Director of Community & Editorial for *Kinder Beauty*. Jasmin was named a "40 Under 40" by The Advocate and her podcast has been honored by The Webby Awards multiple times. She lives in West Hollywood.

**Kanika Sud** is an activist, yoga professional, and sociology professor based in Mumbai. Her activism focuses on drawing parallels between cruelties meted out to womxn under patriarchy and heteronormativity as well as nonhumans under spe-ciesism.

**Lilia Trenkova** is a queer designer, maker, and doer originating from Bulgaria. In 2014, they co-founded the activist group *Collectively Free*, which organized on-the-ground, often high-risk, actions for both nonhuman animal rights and human rights issues through the use of disruptions, street theater, and collaborations. Lilia works as an architectural designer with overlaps from music and set design to food service to permaculture and herbalism. Their inner work currently focuses on healing and transformation—within the context of chosen fami-ly and community.

## Funding Contributors

Deutscher Jugendschutz-Verband

VegFund

# 6 ABOUT SANCTUARY PUBLISHERS

Founded in 2017, Sanctuary Publishers is a Queer, Neurodivergent, BBIPoC-owned and run activism-focused, non-traditional publisher dedicated to resource development in an effort to bridge social justice movements together under the idea of embracing consistent anti-oppression across movements. Since its inception, the publisher has worked to do this through the creation of educational books, websites, booklets, presentations, short videos, and other media. Sanctuary Publishers is committed to giving back and raising the voices of marginalized communities.

**Published Book Titles**

*A Better World Starts Here: Activists and Their Work*

by Stacy Russo

*A Southern Girl's Guide to Plant-Based Eating*

by Cametria Hill

*Baby and Toddler Vegan Feeding Guide*

by Julia Feliz Brueck

*Food Justice: A Primer*

by Saryta Rodriguez

*Veganism in an Oppressive World*

by Julia Feliz Brueck

*Veganism of Color*

by Julia Feliz Brueck

*Wild and Free*

by Andrea Zimmer

**Web Resources**

NewPrideFlag.com

ConsistentAntiOppression.com

VeganismOfColor.com

NeuroAbleism.com

...and much more...

## Further Details

SanctuaryPublishers.com

Printed in Poland
by Amazon Fulfillment
Poland Sp. z o.o., Wrocław

60550686R00197